the first-time founder's

equity bible

gerry hays + ashton chaffee

the first-time founder's

equity bible

gerry hays + ashton chaffee

CONTENTS

FOREWORD

I'll be the first to say it: this book should be required reading for every first-time founder.

As a serial entrepreneur, Gerry Hays has learned first-hand what really matters not only in terms of building a successful business, but with respect to the subject matter at hand: raising capital. He's an educator and mentor who cares deeply about helping others achieve their dreams, and knows what works and what doesn't when it comes to teaching others to successfully work with the principles of equity (myself included).

Because of this, I have no doubt that you too will enjoy and learn much from this book's practical approach to defining and outlining the capital-raising process. Its direct, yet light-hearted tone makes it easier for a first-time entrepreneur to dig into the material, while the illustrative real-world examples make it relatable, aiding in practical application of the lessons presented.

You'll come away from reading this text feeling inspired and more confident in pursuing your entrepreneurial ambitions…an exciting pursuit in which I wish you wild success.

Jared Golden
Founder

AUTHOR'S NOTE

This book would not have happened without Ashton.

I may have laid the foundation for the book and its teachings but the finishing is what everyone sees and that's all on her. Notwithstanding her excellent writing skills, over the past three years, she has learned first-hand the trials and tribulations first-time founders face when launching and building a business, as well as the challenges of raising equity and managing a cap table that come along with it.

It made her a perfect partner on this project, and I hope we continue to partner on future books.

-G

EXCITING TIMES

Being part of a startup team is exciting – the potential for creating the "next big thing" and changing the way the world operates is an experience that cannot be replicated anywhere else.

However, what many entrepreneurs don't realize is that starting and building a successful business isn't all about the idealistic lifestyle portrayed in *The Social Network* or *Entrepreneur* – taking a business towards profitability and, eventually, exit is a long and tough road. Outside of building a product and acquiring customers, founders of high-potential startups face the arduous task of managing founder's equity. Raising capital can be just as time-consuming and stressful as building the business itself, so it's not something to be taken lightly.

Whether it's due to raising capital or granting options to employees, any start-up team with a game-changing idea will end up issuing a good portion of the company's equity (also known as ownership) during the formative stages of the company. For example, Instagram (with less than 20 employees) raised nearly $60 million in equity capital before its acquisition by Facebook[i]…meaning that people outside of the founding team (the people that invested in the company) purchased $60 million worth of the company. Because investors need to be compensated with equity for the risk they've taken on, employees of high-potential ventures may own just 10-20% of the company by the time there's a liquidity event. While issuing equity can dramatically affect the equity of the founders, the loss in ownership may not be inherently negative if enough value is created.

Unfortunately, most first-time entrepreneurs don't understand the capital raising process. In fact, many end up either failing miserably at managing their equity or are surprised when they realize they've agreed to unfavorable investment terms.[1] Much of this confusion can be avoided through understanding the whys and the whens of equity capital financing and issuing stock options.

The First-Time Founder's Equity Bible is designed to give you a high-level understanding of what is an extremely complicated process. Throughout the book, we'll follow co-founders Mike and Sara as they navigate the startup / capital-raising process. Although it won't teach you the nuances of deals or how to negotiate an investment, it will provide you with enough insights into the process to know what questions to ask your attorney, to no longer be intimated by certain deal terms, and, most importantly, to go into the capital formation process with your eyes wide open.

We've found that, in general, most people say "no" to an opportunity either out of fear (because they don't fully understand it) or because they understand the downsides of saying "yes." We hope this book will not only teach you the difference between the two, but will also give you the tools to win when it comes to equity transactions.

*Note: please consult with your attorney before making any of the "big" decisions we discuss in the text. This book is meant to serve as a comprehensive overview of and guide to the process of raising capital for the first time...it is not meant to serve as legal counsel. Deal terms will depend on your unique business offering, the financial climate, and the investors you engage with.

1. For example, it's possible that a founder can own 75% of the total equity but only receive 10% of the cash upon a buyout.

CHAPTER 1
FOUNDER'S EQUITY

Outside of deciding with whom to partner in your new venture, figuring out how to split founder's shares between the team - and fully documenting that split - is perhaps the biggest decision you'll make early in the life of your company.

Let's take a look at Mike and Sara, founders of MealNow, to see how they dealt with this decision:

Mike and Sara are professional acquaintances. At a networking event, they begin talking startups, and Mike tells Sara about a great idea he has – a dinner delivery on-demand company called MealNow. Coincidentally, Sara has been thinking of starting something similar for quite some time. After comparing ideas further, the two decide to partner.

Upon formation of MealNow, Mike and Sara split the ownership 50/50 – that's what's fair, right? Mike has a secure position at Goldman Sachs and would like to continue earning a base salary during the bootstrapping phase, so he decides to wait until MealNow secures adequate funding before jumping "all-in." Sara, on the other hand, is ready to make MealNow a reality, and devotes 100% of her time to launching and running the company.

After a few months, Mike is offered a promotion at Goldman Sachs and decides to stay… putting the responsibility of building the company fully on Sara. However, the two keep their ownership at a 50/50 split because that's what they agreed on at the beginning of the venture.

Over the next seven years, Sara first works without salary, then pays herself a survival amount. With only occasional support from Mike, she builds the company to meaningful revenue, hires a team, and raises the requisite capital to fuel MealNow's growth. Through dramatic ups and downs, Sara is eventually compensated $125,000 a year as the CEO of a 30-person company spanning 10 cities. Meanwhile, Mike is comfortably earning $300,000 a year at Goldman.

At the end of the seventh year, MealNow is acquired by OpenTable for $50 million…a huge success!

MealNow's founder's shares are worth $20MM after paying off investors and employee options. Because of the 50/50 ownership, Sara receives $10MM for her hard work over the past seven years...and so does Mike (even though, relative to Sara, he contributed very little to the company's success).

This situation presents an important question: is a co-founder that provides an idea but doesn't execute on a meaningful level worthy of holding onto a major chunk of equity? The answer, we believe, is NO!

In the following pages, we'll talk about how to avoid the 50/50 fallacy and make sure your founder's shares are distributed appropriately from the beginning.

founder's shares
shares of stock that
are issued to the
founders of a firm.

The decision of how to partition **founder's shares** between the founding team will have lasting consequences for everyone involved: equity determines how much financial benefit each person on your founding team is able to reap upon a liquidity event of the company.

For example, if you create a company with massive value (such as Facebook), even 1% ownership can be worth millions of dollars.[ii] However, only 20 US technology companies reach $100 million+ valuations in any given year.[iii] Buyouts of less than $10-20 million are far more realistic for most entrepreneurs. In this scenario, founders will need to hold a sizeable amount of equity to see a large financial reward from the buyout of their company.

Because of this, it is very important to hold onto as much founder's equity as possible…so **don't take the founder's equity split discussion decision lightly!**

1.1 THE FOUNDER'S EQUITY DISCUSSION

equity
the value of
ownership in a
property, i.e. a
business

First-time entrepreneurs are notorious for avoiding hard discussions on **equity** for fear that it will create hard feelings among the co-founders and ultimately affect morale and dedication. However, these discussions need to take place early in the life of the venture in order to avoid harder, more emotion-fueled discussions later. Relationships can be burned over founder shares (just do a little digging on the story of Snapchat's founding team to see what we mean), so if you want to position your team for long-term success in terms of working relationships, build trust by getting the hard stuff out of the way as soon as you can.

Although it may be convenient and expedient, arbitrarily dividing the equity evenly among founders doesn't usually make sense. If your founding team is not balanced in terms of commitment to the venture and what each person brings to the table, it's important to make sure that those differences are reflected in the issuance of founder's equity. So, before you and your co-founders have the "founder's equity split" discussion, look around the proverbial table and ask yourself:

- Going forward, what value will each person bring to the project?
- Who will develop new products, ideas, features, or uses?
- Who will create or build the product?
- Who will lead the company as CEO?
- Is anyone bringing capital to the table?
- Who has connections to potential funding sources and/or early customers?

The key here is to understand what each founder's contribution is, and to value it appropriately. Although it is a tricky process, there are some general concepts that you can apply to valuing contribution and deciding upon a fitting founder's equity distribution:

1. **The founders that intend to drive the business long-term (you should measure this commitment in years not months) should receive the larger chunk of the equity.** Not surprisingly, the founders that show up and do the work are the people most deserving of equity. Investments, ideas, and connections to capital are great (and clearly necessary), but there is no replacement for digging in and getting things done. You want the individuals that are committed to the business long-term to feel incentivized for their hard work.

2. **Part-time founders and non-performing founders should expect very little equity.** These two groups include people that do not fully invest their time or talents into the company (like Mike in our example), but expect to have a say in decisions. They occasionally provide value, but have outside commitments that take them away from the business on a regular basis. Many times, these founders end up being more of a distraction and drain on the company than anything else!

   However, there are situations when part-timers should be more highly compensated. If part-timers provide valuable strategic guidance, have robust and applicable networks, or deliver on specific work lines, then equity compensation is in order. For example, a strategic advisor would be considered a part-timer, but he or she theoretically brings unrivaled value in terms of helping to grow the business (outside of a monetary investment). Hence, they expect to receive equity for the value, expertise, and connections they add to the business.

3. **Early cash is valuable.** Risk is the highest when the startup is in its earliest stages. Any co-founder that invests cash should expect to receive a decent portion of equity for their investment.

1.2 PROTECTING YOUR SHARES

There's more to founder's ownership than just deciding on how to split up the shares, though. You also need to know how to protect your piece of the pie over time.

We'll assume that you've picked your co-founding team wisely – that you have complementary skills to one another, that you have a shared vision, and that you have the same level of commitment. In the beginning, there is an assumption that each founder will deliver on the value he or she promised. However, sometimes these founding relationships – like many others – don't work out, no matter how much you may want them to. Sometimes, not all founders will perform as promised. Other times, it might be that a certain co-founder won't be able to scale with the business, while still others will be a distraction as they become increasingly difficult to work with.

So, what can you do to minimize the negative impacts if one your co-founders (who holds a large portion of equity) does not work out and ends up leaving the company?

To hedge against these situations, all co-founders should vest their equity. **Vesting** can help solve performance problems down the road, as it naturally deals with dysfunctional or non-committed co-founders.

The way vesting works is that founders must essentially "earn" their equity over time. Although the founders will receive their **pro-rata** share of equity at the beginning of the start-up's life, they will have to earn that equity as they deliver value to the company. A vesting schedule typically lasts four years, with each founder earning his or her equity in equal amounts over that period of time. If one of the founders leaves early (among other unforeseen circumstances), the **Repurchase Agreement** states that the startup has the right to buy

vesting
the accrual of non-forfeitable rights to ownership over a pre-determined period of time

pro-rata
proportionate allocation of a quantity on the basis of one common factor (ex: profit is divided among stockholders on the basis of how many shares each holds)

repurchase agreement
agreement allowing the startup to buy back ownership at a later date for a nominal amount

that founder's equity back for a negligible amount of money.

Let's look at how vesting could help Mike and Sara:

EXAMPLE 1.1

Mike and Sara agree to issue a total of 2,000,000 founder's shares, divide the shares equally between themselves (in other words, split them 50/50), and vest their equity over a four-year period. Because the vesting period is four years and equity is earned in equal amounts each year, each founder earns 25% of their portion of the equity each year:

$$\frac{100\% \text{ of personal equity share}}{4 \text{ years}} = \frac{25\% \text{ of personal equity}}{\text{earned per year}}$$

However, Mike walks away after one year. Because he worked through one vesting period, he only earns (and is able to keep) the 25% portion of his equity that has vested.

To figure out how much of MealNow Mike owns after one year, multiply his original share of ownership in the company by the amount vested:

$$1,000,000 \text{ founder's shares} * 25\% \text{ vested} \quad = \quad 250,000 \text{ shares of MealNow}$$

$$\frac{250,000 \text{ shares owned}}{2,000,000 \text{ total founder's shares}} = \frac{12.5\% \text{ of founder's shares}}{\text{owned}}$$

In year seven, MealNow is sold to OpenTable for $50 million. $20 million of the proceeds go to the common shareholders (including founders).

What payout will Mike receive when MealNow sells, supposing the buyout equates to $8.50 per share bought out?

$$\textbf{Vested shares} \times \textbf{Buyout Price per Share} = \textbf{Payout}$$

$$250,000 \text{ shares} \times \$8.50 = \$2,125,000$$

What payout will Sara receive for her 100% vested founder's shares?

$$1,000,000 \text{ shares} \times \$8.50 = \$8,500,000$$

As you can see, vesting is a protecting and motivating factor for founders.

If you aren't sold on the benefits of vesting (you'd rather every founder have all of their equity today with no strings attached), be aware that if you raise capital from a VC, the fund will most likely require all founders to enter into a vesting agreement with the company. VC's do not want to invest millions into a business where founders have the option to walk away from the startup with 100% of their equity in pocket. Instead, VC's want founders to pledge their equity as collateral so they stay focused on building the company.

Don't be surprised when investors require a vesting agreement. Instead, set this expectation with your co-founders from the start!

KEY TAKEAWAYS

- Have the hard discussion of founder's equity distribution with your team in the early stages of business formation.

- Don't arbitrarily divide equity between the founders in equal amounts – understand each co-founder's contribution and value it appropriately. If your equity split ends up being equal between all parties, that is perfectly okay...just be sure there is a reason behind it!

- Vesting can protect your equity from non-performing co-founders. Create a Founder's Vesting Agreement from the beginning to account for co-founders that don't work out.

CHAPTER 2
ISSUING EQUITY: THE CAP TABLE & DILUTION

After a few years of bootstrapping MealNow, Mike and Sara think they're ready to start talking with various types of investors to infuse some capital into the company to take it to the next level.

Although they believe that raising money is the right thing for the company, the whole process – and thought of "giving up" a part of their business – is making them nervous. This is the first time that Mike and Sara have had to think about issuing equity outside of the core team, and they have a lot to learn.

Mike and Sara have agreed on founder's shares and a vesting schedule, but they haven't set anything in stone on a capitalization table. (Mistake! Document the division of equity for your company as early as possible.) In fact, they aren't really even sure how to set one up. But, they do know that it is an important document that investors want to see, as it clearly demonstrates a company's history of ownership.

Let's follow Sara and Mike as they learn how to create a cap table that not only illustrates to investors who has claim to MealNow's equity, but also accommodates any type of investment into or equity issuance from MealNow.

---

* This statement bears repeating: if you worry about maintaining complete control over the business, you should not raise money from investors. If you raise equity capital, you should be singularly driven to increase the overall valuation of the company, not maintain control over "your baby." Circumstances and performance should drive the decisions, not personal preferences.

2.1 THE CAPITALIZATION TABLE - AN OVERVIEW

The **capitalization table (cap table)** is a detailed summary of who has a claim to equity in a company. At the end of the day, it may include founders, investors, employees, advisors, and board members – anyone who holds a claim to equity will have a place on the cap table.

The cap table is typically one of the first documents that an interested investor or acquiring company will want to look at. This single document lists a great deal of important information, including:

- Major stockholders of the company
- Major option holders of the company (as well as which types of options are held)
- Classes of stock and how much was paid for each class
- How much of each class of stock was bought by each investor, and how many shares of that class the investor owns as a result
- A calculation of ownership on a **fully-diluted** basis[1]

Given that this may be one of the most important documents for your company, you will want to know it inside and out. That's why, although there are hundreds of cap table spreadsheet templates flying around on the Internet, the following examples will teach you how to build a cap table from scratch.

As your company matures, the cap table will become increasingly complicated. However, if you know the basic tenants and setup of the document, you will be able to read and understand even the most complex cap table.

2.2 ISSUING EQUITY

Before you can create an accurate cap table, you must understand the process of issuing equity in a company.

Many first-time entrepreneurs mistakenly think that issuing equity to another party means that, as a founder, you transfer shares from your "bucket" of ownership to the other person. This is not so. Think about it for a minute: if you transfer (i.e. sell) some of your shares, you would personally receive the compensation instead of the company receiving an investment.

Instead, when a company wants to issue equity to new investors or employees, the company will create a new *pool* of equity.

This process of issuing additional shares begins with consulting the company's organizational and operational documents,[2] which regulate the approvals that are required for issuing a new pool of equity. Issuing new equity also usually requires approval by the **Board of Directors** (or the managers, if your startup is an LLC), plus a majority approval of at least 50% of the total outstanding common equity holders. It would be a good idea to secure the help of your attorney during this process in order to ensure it runs smoothly and nothing is overlooked.

---

capitalization table shows who owns what in the company, listing the company's shareholders, the amount of shares they hold, and how much they paid for those shares, in order of decreasing liquidity preference

fully-diluted calculation of the shareholder's percent ownership after all possible shares have been issued

board of directors governing body of a firm. The members are elected by the shareholders and have ultimate decision-making authority

1. This includes options and warrants, whether issued or non-issued, vested or non-vested.

2. For a corporation, consult the by-laws. For an LLC, consult the Operating Agreement.

Each time you issue a new pool of equity, it must be accounted for separately in the cap table. This structure allows an investor to see when the pool was created, how many shares were added, and who received the equity. If equity is issued during a funding round, designate the type of equity issued as well as the price per share. This will allow the investor to see how previous investors priced the company upon their investment.

CALCULATING SHARES ISSUED

Calculating the number of shares issued upon creation of a new equity pool is fairly straightforward, using this equation:

$$\text{\# of Shares in New Equity Pool} = \frac{\text{Total Current Outstanding Shares}^{3}}{(1 - \text{Size of New Pool})} - \text{Total Outstanding Shares}$$

3. This includes any claim to the equity; i.e. shares, warrants, securities, etc.

Pay special attention to the process in the examples below – this same equation is used every time you issue a new equity pool for your startup, regardless of the type or class of equity issued.

EXAMPLE 2.1

Suppose Mike and Sara each own 450,000 founder's shares of MealNow (900,000 shares in total). They want to sell 10% of the company to Investor A. To do this they will have to issue a new pool of shares. How many shares do they issue to Investor A?

Plug the values into the formula, and solve:

# of New Pool Shares	??
Total Current Outstanding Shares	900,000
Size of New Pool	10%

$$\text{New Equity Pool Shares} = \frac{900,000}{(1 - .10)} - 900,000$$

$$\text{New Equity Pool Shares} = 100,000 \text{ new shares}$$

In this case, they would authorize and issue an equity pool size of 100,000 new shares to be transferred to the investor.

EXAMPLE 2.2

Now, suppose that Mike and Sara initially own 758,000 and 730,000 shares of MealNow, respectively. An investor is offering to purchase 13% of the company. How many new shares must MealNow issue?

$$\text{New Equity Pool Shares} \ = \ \frac{1,488,000}{(1 - .13)} \ - \ 1,488,000$$

$$\text{New Equity Pool Shares} \ = \ 222,344 \text{ new shares}$$

Mike and Sara need to issue 222,344 new shares for the investor's 13% share of ownership.

DILUTION

As you may have realized, high-potential startups must often use equity to attract investors and employees. As such, ownership **dilution** is a natural part of the growth process. Remember, each time new pools of equity are issued, it's dilutive to the existing equity holders.

Dilution seems like a dirty word to many first-time entrepreneurs. Nothing good could come out of the fact that the founders' percentage ownership is reduced by issuing a new equity pool and granting shares to investors and employees...right?

Wrong! You may be surprised to learn that dilution isn't always necessarily a bad thing!

Many times, the value of ownership can increase by issuing equity. This would be considered good dilution. Let's take a look:

dilution
occurs for any event that requires the company to issue more shares; equity stake decreases in proportion to the percent of the company new investors buy

EXAMPLE 2.3

Look back at *Example 2.2*, where Sara and Mike issued 222,344 new shares to the investor for 13% of the company.

Let's suppose that when Mike and Sara founded the company, their shares were worth $.01 each, meaning they held $7,580 and $7,300 in value, respectively. However, Investor A paid $1 per share to acquire 13% of the company (in other words, Investor A has agreed to invest $222,344 in order to acquire 13% of MealNow). How much has Mike and Sara's value in ownership increased due to the new per share price?

New Share Price / Old Share Price = Multiple of Increase or Decrease

$$\$1.00 \ / \ \$.01 = 100$$

In *Example 2.3*, Mike and Sara's ownership increased in value 100 times! This means that, based on this valuation, their respective ownerships are valued at $758,000 and $730,000.

price-based dilution
when shares of stock are sold at a price per share that is less than the price paid by earlier investors

At this point, the dilution discussion becomes one of semantics – while the ownership percentage for each founder decreases, the value of the equity held increases. Which would you rather have: a large percentage of something worth less, or a smaller percentage of something worth a lot? That's what we thought!

In contrast, bad dilution (or **price-based dilution**) occurs when both the percent ownership and the value of said ownership decrease as a result of creating a new equity pool. Bad dilution is the result of a **down round**, and can serve as a red-flag to many potential investors.

EXAMPLE 2.4

Instead of $.01, suppose that Mike and Sara each invested capital into MealNow equivalent to $0.20 per share upon formation of the company. Based on this valuation, Mike's ownership is valued at $151,600 (51% ownership) and Sara's ownership is valued at $146,000 (49% ownership)

Mike's Ownership:

758,000 shares x $0.20/share = $151,600

Sara's Ownership:

730,000 shares x $0.20/share = $146,000

Eighteen months later, they run out of money and need an investor to come in. The investor offers to acquire shares of the company at $0.15 per share. Here's how the investment affects Mike and Sara:

Mike:

758,000 shares x $0.15 per share = $113,700
$151,600 - $113,700 = **$37,900** in lost value

Sara:

730,000 shares x $0.15 per share = $109,500
$146,000 - $109,500 = **$36,500** in lost value

In addition to losing close to $40,000 in value each, Mike and Sara's percent ownership is also diluted. No part of this investment is a win!

---

down round
when a company raises money at a lower valuation or share price than in a previous round; existing shareholders lose value

2.3 CREATING THE CAP TABLE

Now that you understand a little more about how to issue equity and the various ways in which dilution can affect the value that you hold, let's begin to build a cap table for Mike and Sara to use as they go through the capital raising process.

But first, here are a few formulas you'll need to keep handy:

$$\text{Share Price} = \frac{\text{Amount Invested}}{\text{Number Shares Issued}}$$

$$\text{Fully-Diluted Ownership \%} = \frac{\text{Total Shares Owned}}{\text{Total Outstanding Claims to Equity}}$$

share price
same as price paid per share; in successful companies, it increases as the company becomes more valuable

liquidation preference
the order in which creditors are paid off if the business is liquidated

*Note: Each time you create a new pool of equity, it should be displayed on the cap table in order of investor and **liquidation preference**.*

EXAMPLE 2.5

Building a Cap Table, Event 1: Founding the Company

Mike and Sara start MealNow, each investing $10,000 in exchange for 500,000 founder's shares. List their number of shares, share price paid, and percent ownership on the new cap table.

Step 1 - Find the **share price**.

$$\text{Share Price} = \frac{\text{Amount Invested}}{\text{Number Shares Issued}}$$

$$\text{Share Price} = \frac{\$20,000}{1,000,000} = \$.02 \text{ per share}$$

Step 2 - Find the fully-diluted ownership percentage:

$$\text{Fully-Diluted Ownership \%} = \frac{\text{Total Shares Owned}}{\text{Total Outstanding Claims to Equity}}$$

$$\text{Fully-Diluted Ownership \%} = \frac{500,000}{1,000,000} = 50\%$$

EXAMPLE 2.5 CONT.

Step 3 - Place values into the cap table:

Round	Founders	% Ownership
Security Type	Common	
Share Price	$0.02	
Mike	500,000	50%
Sara	500,000	50%
Total Shares	1,000,000	1,000,000

EXAMPLE 2.6

Building a Cap Table, Event 2: Friends and Family Round

Sara's parents invest $200,000 into MealNow in exchange for 10% of the company. The new equity pool issued is in common stock.

Step 1 - Find the number of shares issued (introduced on page 22):

$$\text{New Equity Pool} \quad = \quad \frac{1,000,000}{(1 - .10)} \quad - \quad 1,000,000 \quad = \quad 111,111 \text{ shares}$$

Step 2 - Find the share price:

$$\text{Share Price} \quad = \quad \frac{\$200,000}{111,111} \quad = \quad \$1.80 \text{ per share}$$

Step 3 - Find the fully-diluted ownership percentage:

$$\text{Fully-Diluted Ownership \%} \quad = \quad \frac{500,000}{1,111,111} \quad = \quad 45\% \text{ each for Mike and Sara}$$

EXAMPLE 2.6 CONT.

Step 4 - Place values into the cap table:

Round	F & F	Founders	% Ownership
Security Type	Common	Common	
Share Price	$1.80	$0.02	
Mike		500,000	45%
Sara		500,000	45%
Parents	111,111		10%
Total Shares	111,111	1,000,000	1,111,111

EXAMPLE 2.7

Building a Cap Table, Event 3: Angel Round

Six months later, Dave, an angel investor, invests $300,000 in MealNow in exchange for 8% of the company. The type of security issued is **convertible preferred stock**.

Step 1 - Find the number of shares issued:

$$\text{New Equity Pool} = \frac{1,111,111}{(1 - .08)} - 1,111,111 = 96,618 \text{ shares}$$

Step 2 - Find the share price:

$$\text{Share Price} = \frac{\$300,000}{96,618} = \$3.11 \text{ per share}$$

Step 3 - Find the fully-diluted ownership percentage for each equity holder:

$$\text{Fully-Diluted Ownership \%} = \frac{500,000}{1,207,729} = 41.4\% \text{ each for Mike and Sara}$$

$$\text{Fully-Diluted Ownership \%} = \frac{111,111}{1,207,729} = 9.2\% \text{ for parents}$$

convertible preferred stock
preferred stock that can be converted into common stock at the option of the stockholder (see Ch. 6 for more discussion)

EXAMPLE 2.7 CONT.

Step 4 - Place values into the cap table:

Round	Angel / Seed	F & F	Founders	% Ownership
Security Type	Convertible	Common	Common	
Share Price	$3.11	$1.80	$0.02	
Mike			500,000	41.40%
Sara			500,000	41.40%
Parents		111,111		9.20%
Angel Dave	96,618			8.00%
Total Shares	96,618	111,111	1,000,000	1,207,729

EXAMPLE 2.8

Building a Cap Table, Event 4: Series A

option pool
shares set aside
for possible
issuance to
employees at a
later date

strike price
the price at
which an option
is exercisable

Two years later, Julie – a VC – wants to invest $5 million in exchange for 35% of the company. However, Julie wants Mike and Sara to create a 10% **option pool** alongside her investment (for more information on this topic and how it affects valuation, see Chapter 4). The **strike price** of the options will be the same price per share paid by Julie.

Step 1 - Find the number of shares issued:

To create the new equity pool (which will be divided between Julie and the options pool), the company will have to issue enough shares to be equivalent to 45% of the company, fully diluted:

$$\text{New Equity Pool} = \frac{1,207,729}{(1 - .45)} - 1,207,729 = 988,142 \text{ shares}$$

Allocate these new shares appropriately between Julie (35%) and the option pool (10%):

35% / 45% = 78% of the new shares go to Julie
.78 x 988,142 shares = **770,751** shares for Julie

10% / 45% = 22% of the new shares go to the options pool
.22 x 988,142 = **217,391** shares for the options pool

EXAMPLE 2.8 CONT.

Step 2 - Find the share price (based on the price Julie pays for her portion of the shares):

$$\text{Share Price} = \frac{\$5,000,000}{770,751} = \$6.48 \text{ per share}$$

Step 3 - Find the fully-diluted ownership percentage for each equity holder:

$$\text{Fully-Diluted Ownership \%} = \frac{500,000}{2,195,871} = 23\% \text{ each for Mike and Sara}$$

$$\text{Fully-Diluted Ownership \%} = \frac{111,111}{2,195,871} = 5\% \text{ for parents}$$

$$\text{Fully-Diluted Ownership \%} = \frac{96,618}{2,195,871} = 4\% \text{ for Angel Dave}$$

Step 4 - Place values into the cap table:

Round	Series A	Angel / Seed	F & F	Founders	Options	% Ownership
Security Type	Participating	Convertible	Common	Common	Common	
Share Price	$6.48	$3.11	$1.80	$0.02	$6.48	
Mike				500,000		23%
Sara				500,000		23%
Parents			111,111			5%
Angel Dave		96,618				4%
VC Julie	770,751					35%
Option Pool					217,391	10%
Total Shares	770,751	96,618	111,111	1,000,000	217,391	2,195,871

Note: Remember that the cap table is set up in order of liquidity from left to right. Because of this, the "options" column is placed to the right of founder's shares. Options that are exercised will become common shares.

EXAMPLE 2.9

Building a Cap Table, Event 5: Equity to Employees

Mike and Sara decide to hire a new CTO. They grant the new hire options equivalent to 1% of the company.

Step 1 - Find the number of shares transferred to CTO from the options pool:

Shares to Transfer = Total Number of Shares x Desired % Ownership

$$\text{Shares to Transfer} = 2{,}195{,}871 \times .01$$
$$\text{Shares to Transfer} = 21{,}958 \text{ shares}$$

Step 2 - Find the shares remaining in unallocated options pool:

Shares in Options Pool - Shares Transferred = Shares Remaining

$$217{,}391 - 21{,}958 = 195{,}433 \text{ shares in options pool}$$

Step 3 - To show this on the cap table, simply move the amount from the unallocated options pool to a new row created for the CTO. This adjustment does not impact any of the other equity holders, as a new equity pool has not been created.

Round	Series A	Angel / Seed	F & F	Founders	Options	% Ownership
Security Type	Participating	Convertible	Common	Common	Common	
Share Price	$6.48	$3.11	$1.80	$0.02	$6.48	
Mike				500,000		23%
Sara				500,000		23%
Parents			111,111			5%
Angel Dave		96,618				4%
VC Julie	770,751					35%
CTO					21,958	1%
Option Pool					195,433	9%
Total Shares	770,751	96,618	111,111	1,000,000	217,391	2,195,871

Note: issuing warrants to advisors or board members works the same way as issuing employee options.

Issuing equity can be a tricky – and, let's face it, emotional – process. But with the right tools in hand, you'll be able to navigate the process a little more easily.

KEY TAKEAWAYS

- The cap table is an important document that you should know inside and out before you talk with investors…it's a detailed history of your company's capitalization.

- Each time you issue a new pool of equity, it must be accounted for on the cap table.

- Dilution is a natural part of a startup's life. Don't be afraid of it. While bad dilution does exist, good dilution can actually increase the value you hold.

CHAPTER 3
GET YOUR MIND RIGHT:
PREPPING FOR INVESTOR INTERACTIONS

Now that they know the ins and outs of issuing equity, Mike and Sara are feeling good about trying to raise capital. MealNow already has great traction with both customers and restaurants…but they just need a little more capital to keep up with development demands.

Unfortunately, Mike and Sara still don't understand some of the basic practices of engaging with investors…should they be seeking debt or equity capital? How much should they be asking for from various sources? And is there anything they need to know about pitching to investors?

From different types of financing to the appropriate raise ranges by stage, let's take a look at some of the areas Mike and Sara will need to be familiar with before engaging with their investor network.

Plan on reading this chapter through a few times before you begin speaking with investors about raising equity capital for your startup. While it is not exhaustive of all topics, this chapter is a "catch-all" for many of the things you need to understand at a high-level before approaching investors.

3.1 DEBT VS EQUITY CAPITAL: AN IMPORTANT DISTINCTION

Many first-time founders confuse debt and equity capital when it comes to investment terms. However, the two have very different implications and sit at opposite ends of the risk spectrum. There is also a third in-between option that is becoming increasingly prevalent in earlier stage capital infusions which combines the best of both instruments.

Debt capital is similar to any other type of loan; with debt capital, you have an obligation to repay an investor the loaned sum plus a fee to use the investor's money (in the form of an interest rate). Just like with other forms of debt, there is a deadline to repay the loan plus interest (for example, 12 months up to several years). The investor loaning the money will most likely want to secure his or her loan by taking **a lien** on company assets. Thus, if the company isn't able to repay the loan, and the loan is secured by the assets, the investor will have a right to liquidate the company's assets to recoup his or her investment.

debt capital
borrowing someone else's money to finance the business under the condition that the money (plus interest accrued) must be paid back in full by an agreed upon date in the future

If you receive debt capital from a bank, you will most likely have to sign a personal guarantee stating that if the business cannot repay the loan, you will repay the loan personally. In a worst-case scenario, this can result in personal bankruptcy.

While those potential financial repercussions can be scary, there are some benefits to raising debt capital. Debt investors do not benefit from soaring profits or major appreciation of your company's stock, and are therefore only concerned with securing the value of their loan plus interest accrued. Because the investor has no claim to (or, really, interest in) the profits of the business, they hold no power in telling you how to run your business.

lien
a legal claim to another person's property

Businesses with customers and profits – typically more mature companies – are usually the only companies eligible for debt financing, making debt financing significantly less risky for investors.

If you are a founder that needs capital to build and unlock the value of a new product or service (in other words, your business is virtually unproven in the market), debt financing will not be available to you – equity financing will be the best path to securing the funds you need to build your company. However, this is a much riskier path for investors for two reasons: the products and services have not been proven, and equity is paid out only after all debts have been settled.

Equity capital represents ownership in the company. When investors have ownership in the company, they have an interest in the ultimate outcome of the business – the more profitable and successful the business is, the more money they get out of it.

equity capital
represents the risk capital staked by investors through investment in the company

Because of the increased amount of risk paired with the high potential returns, investors with equity capital usually want to have a say in how things are run. As such, investors will request seats on the Board of Directions or other advisory and voting roles within the company as part of the equity financing agreement.

The dynamic between the Board of Directors and founders can be tension-filled. For example, if you and your founders are doing a poor job of running and growing the company – growth isn't happening as quickly as investors think it should – you can expect equity holders to try and fix things. A common fix is to replace those that are running the company – meaning you and your co-founders could be kicked out of the company you created. However, this is usually a worst-case scenario and can be avoided by fostering trust, creating positive relationships, and executing!

First-time founders usually have the mindset that the business is "their baby." If you raise equity capital, this illusion needs to be dispelled immediately. When investors begin to ask questions and assert power - and they will, if they are at all concerned about protecting their investment and eventually realizing a return - you can't take it personally. Separating your identity from that of the company will only serve you well in the long run, as you'll be better able to make objective decisions, listen to your expert advisors, and avoid common pitfalls that many first-time founders face.

Savvy investors want to back founders that are willing to give up some control, make room for other talented individuals, and ensure that the company rapidly adjusts to fit the market. If you are not willing to do this, you should avoid raising equity capital.

liquidity event
the way in which an investor plans to close out an investment; i.e. an exit strategy. For example, an IPO or acquisition

It is also worth mentioning that investors don't want to hold onto their equity forever – the prime reason that they invested equity capital was for the potential of large returns within a relatively short time period (about 5-10 years). As such, at the time equity capital is raised, the company's trajectory should be singularly pointed towards a **liquidity event.**

If you intend on running your company as a lifestyle business, equity capital isn't for you… you're a prime candidate for debt capital.

However, if you're in the early stages of raising capital - i.e. a friend and family, pre-seed, seed, or in rare cases, maybe even a Series A round - you have a third option to pursue: the **convertible note**.

convertible note
structured as a loan at the time of investment; outstanding balance is automatically converted to equity when a later equity investor appears

Convertible notes combine characteristics of the two instruments discussed above, as convertible notes represent debt capital that is convertible into equity at some point in the future. This conversion typically happens in the next round of priced financing. If you are raising a smaller round or think that landing on a valuation is going to be a challenge (i.e. if you are still at the seed stage and it's too early to place a reliable value on the company), you may consider offering investors convertible notes.

promissory note
document signed by a borrower promising to repay a loan under agreed-upon terms

With this type of security, investors receive a **promissory note** for the amount they invest. The note includes a conversion feature, meaning that upon a **qualified financing** event (i.e. a priced round in which a valuation is placed on the company), the debt will automatically convert into equity at a discount to the valuation negotiated at the time of the qualified financing.

qualified financing
an equity financing in which a minimum amount of capital is raised

This discount rewards the investor for taking early risk. For example, if the discount is set at 20% (10-30% is a common discount range, although discounts to the valuation will vary based on the timing of the investment and your negotiations with the investor), the investor will receive $1.20 worth of shares in the priced round for every $1 lent to the company through the note.

How would a convertible note play out for one of Mike and Sara's investors? Let's look.

EXAMPLE 3.1

Angel Dave wants to invest in Sara's business, but Sara believes it's too early to price the round and sell equity. Angel Dave agrees to invest $100,000 in exchange for a convertible note with a 15% discount and automatic conversion into equity upon Sara raising a minimum of $500,000 in qualified financing.

A year later, Tina the VC invests $1,000,000 in Sara's business at $1.00 per share, receiving participating preferred shares with a 1x return preference. This financing event triggers an automatic conversion of Angel Dave's note, allowing him to purchase the same security as Tina the VC at a 15% discount to her price.

Step 1: Calculate how much Angel Dave will pay per share.

Priced round = $1 per share x 15% discount = $0.15 discount per share
$1 per share - $0.15 per share = $0.85 discount price per share

Step 2: Calculate the number of shares Dave acquires.

Amount Invested / Price Per Share = # Shares Acquired
$100,000 / $0.85 = 117,647 shares

Angel Dave is able to acquire 17,647 more shares than he otherwise would have due to the discount he received. The higher the discount, the more shares Angel Dave will receive.

If you are dealing with investors that bring great value outside of their capital, they may not be so willing to accept a convertible note. When they invest, the value they bring can rapidly accelerate the enterprise value of the company. In this situation, not locking their equity in at a concrete value could cause them to miss out on early equity appreciation. Because of this, some investors will want to **cap** the valuation at a pre-determined price.

The cap is a term that is favorable to investors, as it essentially locks their investment in at a maximum price to ensure they are appropriately rewarded for investing early in the company's life. When the discounted value goes above the cap, the cap is applied to the valuation. However, any valuation up to the cap will results in the investor receiving the discount rate.

This is easier to understand through an example, so let's look at how this might play out with one of Sara and Mike's investors.

convertible with a cap
debt-like investment instrument that converts into equity in the future at a discount to the funding price with a pre-set price maximum

EXAMPLE 3.2

Angel Dave wants to invest $100,000 in MealNow. In his mind, the company's valuation is probably pretty close to $4 million, but he does not go through the process of pricing the round or setting a cap on the convertible note when negotiating with Sara and Mike.

One year later, MealNow raises a Series A round, which is priced at $20 million, pre-money. With a discount of 20%, Angel Dave's investment is priced at valuation of $16 million

EXAMPLE 3.2 CONT.

instead of the $4 million he initially presupposed.

$$\$20 \text{ million } * \text{ } 20\% \text{ discount } = \$4 \text{ million}$$

$$\$20 \text{ million } - \text{ } \$4 \text{ million } = \$16 \text{ million discounted pre-money value}$$

In this scenario, Dave would have benefitted greatly if he had instead invested in MealNow at a priced valuation of $4 million...or, really, anything less than $16 million. Because he did not price the round initially, he lost out on a huge increase in the company's value.

However, suppose Dave agrees to invest in MealNow if his convertible note has a cap. The two parties settle on a $4 million cap with a 20% discount.

If, upon future funding, MealNow is valued at anything up to $5 million, Dave's investment is valued at the discount rate. As noted before, this is because the discounted value of the investment is lower than or equal to the cap (check: $5 million - 20% discount = $4 million).

Once the discounted value of his investment goes above the cap of $4 million (for example if the valuation in the next round is $6 million, his discounted rate is $4.8 million), the cap applies and his investment is priced at the lower amount. At this point, Dave "locks in" the value of his invesment and can secure a higher upside for his initial risk.

So, what if MealNow is valued at $20 million pre-money? Dave's shares will convert in at an effective price of $4 million instead of the $16 million they would have converted at if he did not have the cap in place.

Clearly, the convertible note's value (with or without a cap) to investors is twofold: first, investors don't have to go through the process of coming up with an initial valuation. Second, the investor receives a discount to or cap on the valuation paid by the investors that price the qualified round, meaning that they experience an upside to the investment.

Another benefit of convertible notes - for both parties - is that they can accelerate the process of getting cash into the company in the early stages, enabling you to concentrate on building the business sooner. Since these types of investments typically happen early in the life of a startup, it is usually less of a negotiation process than raising equity capital. There is room to negotiate a bit on discount rates and capped valuations, but just like any other investment, the earlier the stage of the company, the higher the risk...and higher risk translates into a higher discount rate.

There is a healthy debate regarding the use of convertible notes and the value of utilizing a cap, so be sure to check out the endnotes for some valuable resources on the subject.[iv]

3.2 DE-RISKING TO RAISE CAPITAL

First-time founders, by definition, do not have a track record of success to parade in front of investors. However, very few start-ups raise significant amounts of equity capital on nothing more than an idea. Although it's happened on occasion (see *Case Study 3.1*), most investors are leery of deploying capital in pursuit of ideas in the abstract: most investors want to see proof of customer adoption and a large enough future customer pool to make the investment worthwhile.[1]

For this reason, prospective investors will concentrate on the underlying value of opportunity and judge a founder's ability to execute on the vision. These two factors – the right opportunity and the right team in the eyes of the investor – make it quite difficult to raise equity capital.

In order to increase chances of getting funded, founders need to go through the process of **de-risking** their venture.

At the idea stage, there is little certainty in the future of the business. In fact, there are many more questions than answers in this stage. That in and of itself is not what will prohibit you from raising equity capital – investors almost expect that there will be a question / answer imbalance.

That being said, they also expect that you will have spent considerable time and resources (yours and other people's) answering some of those questions before they will be ready to invest in you. Some of the most important questions that you need to be ready to answer or demonstrate include:

- Does the product work?
- Is there a large enough consumer base?
- Is the product **defensible**?
- Is your team the right team for the job?

As you begin to answer these questions, make sure you are doing so in a realistic manner. You will not win (i.e. be funded successfully) by promising big moments, as oftentimes, sweeping promises cannot be delivered upon reliably. The best way to de-risk a company and prove its value in the market is to set realistic, achievable milestones relating to gaining customer traction and improving the product. Investors prefer smaller, tangible, consistent material advances in the company rather than always relying on home-run type movements. If you position your startup with this approach, you will be in a strong position to "**cross the chasm**."

While gaining market acceptance is a primary means of de-risking the company and attracting investors, it is important to remember that because although investors are in the business of taking risk, the risks they take are always highly calculated to give them the best odds of achieving success. It is up to you to prove that investing in your company gives them the chance to do just that!

An important caveat is that risk reduction, just as many other startup processes, will

---

de-risking
process of a creating enough certainty in your company such that it becomes an attractive opportunity to a large pool of investors

defensible
meaningful differentiation in product sets to gain market share, expand margins and keep competitors at bay; ex: competitive advantage, barriers to entry, IP, language

cross the chasm
gaining market share as the company moves from acquiring / serving early adopters to mainstream consumers

1. The only caveat to this is that "proven" founders will have access to VC's at much earlier stages than unproven founders. For example, were Mark Zuckerburg to walk into a room with 20 VC's to pitch a an idea, a decent percentage would (or should) fund the venture on Zuckerburg's ability and talent alone. This is referred to as "betting on the jockey."

CASE STUDY 3.1: THE RISE AND FALL OF COLOR

In early 2011, proximity-based sharing application Color raised $41 million from some of Silicon Valley's biggest names…pre-launch. Some have argued that the large bet placed by the VC's stemmed from a completely new way of thinking about digitally-based social connectivity in the physical world, while others have touted the experience of the founding team.

During the year after its much-hyped launch, though, Color faced several stumbling blocks, including a struggling product and executive departures. Not only did the team have difficulty in unlocking the product – pivoting several times from a photo-sharing app, to a video broadcasting app for Facebook, to partnering with Verizon – but it also didn't function as a team, as its Board of Directors and executives never presented a truly united front.

Not two years after funding, the company began to wind down operations. Apple eventually acquired Color's engineering team and assets for a reported $2-$5 million.[v]

---

accelerator
privately-funded early stage investment fund that supports entrepreneurs with funding, mentoring, training, development events, and access to a premier investor network for a definite period of time in exchange for equity

require some capital. If you are in the position where you need to raise capital in order to do this, though, be sure to raise an appropriate amount. Just as with any other round, you want to raise an amount that will materially advance the business, answer enough questions to prove out the opportunity, and position the company to attract future investor. But remember: too much capital can be just as dangerous as too little!

3.3 STAGES OF RAISING CAPITAL

bootstrap
building a business out of very little or virtually nothing, keeping costs as low as possible and relying on personal income or savings, sweat equity, low operating costs, fast inventory turnaround; avoiding outside investors so ownership is not diluted

Raising capital for a startup often falls along a specific timeline. Many first-time founders make the mistake of going after any money they can get…a practice that is a waste of time (for many reasons). Each round should be priced in a way that does not lead to adverse selection in filling out the rest of the round or in future rounds. This means that rounds need to be priced in a way where the best potential investors for your company are excited and willing to participate. Don't alienate strategic investors by pricing a round too high just because you can get a larger commitment from others!

The amount of capital you raise – and from whom – will depend highly on what stage of development your company is in. So, if your company is not accepted into an acclaimed **accelerator** program, keep this general blueprint in mind when raising equity capital.

bartering
type of trading in which goods or services are exchanged without the use of cash, used in times of high inflation or tight money

Stage 1: Idea to first customer. As the "birth" stage of your company, this is the time when you should be **bootstrapping** your way to developing a working product and demoing it to your target customers.

Target Raise: $0 - $250,000 in bootstrapped capital

Types of Investors to Pursue: personal funds, **bartering,** family and friends

Hurdles to Raising Money: There are very few hurdles in this stage. Along with your personal capital, family and friends will invest in you because they want to see you succeed. Keep in mind, though, that this doesn't necessarily validate your idea or the market opportunity. Partnerships with other firms play a key role here as well. Trading services or creating monthly retainers can help both sides, as founders can acquire high-quality services at a reduce initial rate, while partners get the benefit of growing their business along with the startup's success. These core relationships can create a solid foundation between partnering companies that grows with time.

Stage 2: Product refinements + getting more customers. During this stage of product development, you should be refining your product based on beta user input. You should be talking to potential customers or users regularly and should have a solid and growing initial user base. This is when you really start to understand and unlock the value of your product / service.

Target raise: $250,000 - $750,000 in seed funds

Types of Investors to Pursue: **Angel Investors**, Seed Stage Venture Funds

angel investors
wealthy individuals operating as informal or private investors who provide venture financing for small businesses

Hurdles to Raising Money: You need to be able to present an actual product to the investors you are talking with (not just a slide deck!). You should be able to talk about the opportunity in the context of existing customers and user traction.

If your customer count is small, your customers should be paying customers in order to make a compelling case. In contrast, if you are pitching a free product, you should have a considerable (and growing) user base to show traction and future opportunity.

Stage 3: Commercialization. During this stage, you will be raising money in order to produce your product at scale.

Target raise: $1,000,000 - $5,000,000

Types of Investors to Pursue: Traditional Venture Funds (**Series A**)

Series A
a company's first significant round of traditional venture capital

Hurdles to Raising Money: At this stage, you need to demonstrate that there is an opportunity for the venture fund to achieve a sizeable return. For instance, VC's usually look for a 20-50x return on the invested capital within a 5-7 year timeframe. As such, your company should have the projected potential to reach $100MM in revenue during that time.

Stage 4: Rapid Commercialization. Your company has some great momentum, but a final round of capital will put you over the hill into profitability.

Target raise: $5,000,000 - $20,000,000

Types of Investors to Pursue: Later Stage Venture Funds (Series B)

Hurdles to Raising Money: Although your company has continued momentum in terms of revenue growth, you must have a line of sight into profitability or have potential for a near-term exit (within 3-5 years).

As you can see, the process of raising capital can be daunting. Because there are so many questions, hurdles and variables within the process, *successful equity financings are extremely difficult to achieve.*[2]

The following are characteristics of successful financings:

- A sufficient amount of capital is raised to take the company to the next logical level - i.e. milestones are achieved and the business has materially progressed.
- Terms and conditions are favorable for both the founders and the investors.
- The funding partners add value to the company outside of the cash they invest.

So, how do you increase your chances of achieving a successful equity financing? Although it may be cliché to advise founders to choose investing partners wisely, capital can be very expensive if the investing partners do not provide value outside of their capital. As a founder, you need to seek investors that materially advance the company in terms of connections to potential partners, customers, and even future investors.

Many times, though, investors will take care of this decision for you: a great number of active investors will pass on the opportunity to invest in your company if they don't feel they can add value past their capital contribution.

If you spend your time reaching out to the investors that best fit your opportunity (based on things like their investment background and industry experience), you're likely not only to increase your chances of securing capital, but to also get some invaluable advice along the way.

*Note: Please remember that every startup is unique and that many factors (including market, industry, individual investors / funds, the founders themselves, among others) will affect how much capital is raised and when. Although this framework for deal progression and size of raises at the various stages is a generally accepted construct, it is by no means the be-all, end-all. Deal terms and sizes are just as unique as the companies they support, so don't fret if your path does not mirror this framework exactly over the life of your company! If you focus on building a fundamentally solid business, investors can and will work with you to structure appropriate deal terms and sizes. For more on the topic of valuation, see Chapter 4.

3.4 PREPARE FOR INVESTOR MEETINGS: UNDERSTAND COGNITIVE BIASES

It's a widely-accepted fact that most parents think their baby is the cutest thing to ever grace the face of the earth, when, in fact, infants all pretty much look the same. Of course, there are always outliers in either direction…but generally, they're all just squishy-faced, tiny humans with no distinct features (cute, nonetheless).

2. Although many founders are able to raise money, not many complete successful equity financings.

Startups, too, are kind of like infants – as founders, you and your team give birth to the idea. You think everyone will love it just as much as you do, that it's revolutionary and an essential improvement upon today's lifestyles, so you devote most all of your time and effort into building it into a real company.

You, just as an infant's parents, have a **bias** towards your creation.

Biases are dangerous: they cloud reality, they blind founders to potential pitfalls and flaws in the business design, and they stymie the inevitable pivots a business must go through.

In order to have effective and successful discussions with investors, you must guard yourself against several of the most common cognitive biases that entrepreneurs face, such as…

Anchoring: Successful entrepreneurs don't become attached to any single bit of information; they constantly look for more information about their product or service's industry and customers so they can rapidly improve the customer experience and the value of the offering. Entrepreneurs that don't have an anchoring bias also maintain a level of pragmatism when it comes to raising money.

Confirmation Bias: Confirmation bias occurs when entrepreneurs seek out evidence to support their preconceived notions about their business idea and market, while ignoring any and all evidence to the contrary. Great entrepreneurs don't look for validation – they look for things that can derail their company and use that knowledge to create a better product.

Optimism Bias: Entrepreneurial over-optimism tends to lead to decisions that can be financially fatal to a company. Investors are wary of entrepreneurs who behave as if nothing bad will ever happen, and instead prefer to see a realistic and cautious optimism: a conviction and passion that the opportunity is ripe, paired with the ability to identify and overcome potential challenges.

Arm yourself against these biases early and check yourself often. By their very nature, biases are difficult to see in yourself. Having an open, honest, and trusting relationship with your co-founders, advisors, and future investors will help to keep everyone in check.

Past overcoming these biases, it is important to "get your mind right" in other ways. When approaching investor meetings, you need to conduct diligence in a manner much like you initially did for the company itself. Get to know potential firms and investors inside and out...look into their personal work history, experiences, and expertise. Study the companies they've invested in, the industries they occupy, and the products they've developed. Try to deduce what stage the product was in when they invested; see if you can dig up any specifics of the deal.

The more you know about an investor, their deal history, their tendencies, and what types of deals or opportunities are most attractive to them, the better you'll be able to prepare your pitch, your questions, and your approach. Don't underestimate the importance of this! Investors expect that you will have done diligence in every aspect of your business...and if it's clear that you haven't, they'll make it known that you're wasting their time (and at that point, a deal will not get done).

There are many other factors that go into preparing for investor interactions, but

bias
inclination or preference that influences judgment from being balanced

anchoring
tendency to rely too heavily on certain pieces of information when making decisions

confirmation bias
tendency to retain only what conforms to one's preferences and reject that which does not

optimism bias
tendency to overestimate favorable outcomes

understanding these principles will help put you in the right frame of mind for approaching investors, ultimately giving you a higher chance of success for securing equity financing.

KEY TAKEAWAYS

- Figuring out what stage your company is in will help you determine whether you should pursue debt or equity capital, how much, and from whom.

- Investors only take calculated risks – work to de-risk your startup for better chances of securing financing.

- Every entrepreneur has a set of cognitive biases. Spend time identifying and eliminating yours before approaching investors.

CHAPTER 4
VALUATION

Sara and Mike have done their diligence on prepping for investor interactions: they know how to structure a cap table, they're confident about issuing equity, they've studied up on risk, and they've begun to rid themselves of the cognitive biases that have been slightly skewing their outlook for the past few months.

However, Sara is having a tough time valuing MealNow. She knows, though, that the valuation is going to play a large role in her discussions with prospective investors, and she needs to be prepared.

In order to enter into negotiations with a strong position (and have an idea of what types of terms investors will want as well as what kind of investment MealNow is seeking), Sara and Mike will have to learn a few key points about calculating valuations against investors' expectations.

Let's take a look at some concepts and formulas Sara and Mike will need to know in order to accurately – and smartly – value MealNow.

4.1 WHAT IS YOUR BUSINESS WORTH?

valuation
appraisal or
estimate of the
worth of the
business

Valuation is undoubtedly one of the biggest hurdles to overcome when negotiating the sale of equity to an investor, as the valuation of the company determines the price of the equity.

Why is this so difficult?

For most early stage companies, nobody really knows what the true current or future value of the startup is. Think of it in terms of the NBA draft: players are drafted and paid based on expected future contributions to the team. In the same way, startups are valued based on the expected future value of the equity. In the end (and much like the professional player), the company has to perform at a high level for the investor to get a return on his or her investment.

Because there is typically no operating history for early-stage startups – in terms of things like paying customers or true market traction – it is important for you to understand a few general principles[1] that investors will take into account when valuing your company.

Note: Many first-time founders spend hours creating complex spreadsheets to demonstrate the perceived future value of the company. Don't waste your time doing this! Because these spreadsheets are based almost entirely on assumptions, they are typically irrelevant to sophisticated investors.

PRINCIPLE 1 - ASSESSING RISK

rate of return
expressed as a
percentage of
the total amount
invested

Building a startup is potentially one of the riskiest things that you can do – the chances of a high-potential venture succeeding in Silicon Valley is literally one in 10,000, according to Steve Blank.

liquidity risk
probability of
loss arising from
a situation where
there will not be
enough cash or
cash equivalents to
meet debts; sale of
illiquid assets will
yield less than their
fair value

As a result, investors need potential returns to cover the high amount of composite risk they take on…meaning that any one investment should be able to offset the losses they experience from a group of other investments that fail to return any capital. This need to "make up" for lost capital dictates an investor's required **Rate of Return (ROR)**. As you might guess, the riskier the investment, the higher the required ROR.

So, how do investors go about calculating their ROR? Below we detail several risk factors that go into the calculation.

Liquidity Risk

Liquidity risk accounts for the likelihood that the company will not be able to raise additional capital following the current round. For example, if there are no customers buying the product or service, and future potential investors do not believe that an additional investment will get the company to the point where it has paying customers (or hits a critical mass of free users), the company will most likely be forced to shut down due to liquidity issues. If this happens, investors will walk away with nothing.

1. These
valuation principles
are based on early
stage companies
with little or no
revenues or profit,
but high potential
for growth and
profitability.

Unfortunately, shutting down due to funding issues or lack of profitability is the fate of the vast majority of startups…particularly those that dramatically increase their **burn rate** with the belief that customers or new investments will be acquired in the near-term. Because of its prevalence, this type of risk is usually weighted more heavily than other forms of risk.

burn rate
speed at which a new firm consumes capital and credit before breaking even and generating income

Market Risk

Most startups that reach a high level of financial success can attribute a portion of their success to "timing the market" – targeting a market segment that grows substantially within a certain timeframe and entering the market at just the right moment (see Chapter 10 for more detail).

Because markets are largely unpredictable, it's almost impossible to know exactly the right time to introduce a product or service, giving rise to **market risk**. However, timing is essential: even the smartest entrepreneurs in the world have a difficult time building a massive company if they time the market incorrectly. Getting your market timing right is oftentimes the difference between massive adoption and early (costly) startup death. It's a tricky balance, as timing affects startups both ways: a company can fail from being either too early for the market or too late to the market (see *Case Study 4.1*).

market risk
probability of loss common to all businesses and investment opportunities and inherent in all dealings in a market

Your market will largely determine the success of your startup. Because the market is so volatile (but important), investors weigh this risk heavily as well.

Management Risk

We've said it before and we'll say it again: launching a company is one of the hardest things a person can do. Because of that, first-time founders will make many mistakes that most seasoned entrepreneurs do not.

CASE STUDY 4.1: TIMING IS EVERYTHING

Much of market timing is based on "hanging around" until rapid adoption occurs. For example, an email marketing company launched in 1995 would have faced multiple challenges achieving adoption as compared to the same type of company launched in 2005. The difference in timing here is obvious: in 1995, very few consumers and businesses used email; by 2005, email had become a ruling factor in our day-to-day lives.

Sometimes, companies can hit the market too early. For example, Nokia came out with the first smart phone in 2004, before many "smart" technologies as we know them today existed. This helped to create and shape the market so that others could successfully introduce their own technologies.[vi]

However, other companies can hit the market too late, creating a need to overcome the entrenched competitors. Microsoft is a prime example - the company is still trying to penetrate the smart phone market. Interestingly, Microsoft acquired Nokia's devices and services division for $7.2 billion.[vii]

management risk
the risks associated with ineffective, destructive or underperforming management, which hurt shareholders and the company or fund being managed. In this situation, the company would be better off without the choices made by management

Some factors that play into **management risk** (particularly for first-time founders) include:

- Members of the founding team often have to wear many hats and fill roles that they may not have core competencies in
- Founders can easily lose track of the many moving parts within a startup
- Startups can be stressful environments rife with infighting and missed opportunities

These are skills that can be mastered through practice and experience...however, gaining that experience can be a rough path. Mistakes that first-time founding teams make can be fatal. With the right guidance and support, though, this risk can be somewhat mitigated, making it a mid-high level risk.

Macro Risks

macro risk
large-scale economic factors that you cannot control (and oftentimes cannot predict) that affect your business in a negative way

Recessions or times of volatility in the markets are examples of **macro risks.** During these times, customers aren't as willing to buy, and purchase orders take longer to come in. To incentivize or spur buying, prices are reduced, which squeezes margins and creates cash constraints. Macro risks have very real implications on new companies, so investors must account for them. However, large scale risks such as these are easier to identify and hedge against, typically giving them the lowest risk rating.

Competitive Risks

competitive risk
the risk that a company cannot ward off competitors before it can return capital to investors

Competitive risk has a lot to do with market timing, but it also relies on the defensible position of the company's product or service – what do you have that differentiates (and protects) you from the competition?

If you cannot ward off the competition long enough to create a profitable return for investors, your company will not be of interest to investors.

Earlier stage companies will have higher probabilities for each type of risk due to all of the unknowns that are intrinsic to startups. Accordingly, later stage startups (Series A and B rounds) will theoretically have lower risk in each of the categories.

Sophisticated investors typically make a probability judgment (whether consciously or not) and assign each type of risk a value to weigh it, then combine these probabilities to find their required ROR (see *Table 4.1* as an illustrative example).

Risk Probabilities	
Funding / Liquidity Risk	15%
Market Risk	15%
Management Risk	10%
Macro Risks	5%
Competitive Risks	15%
Required ROR	60%

Because the degree of risk should decrease with each round of financing, investments in later rounds will also typically require a smaller ROR, as shown in *Table 4.2*.

Expected Returns	
Angel / Seed Funds	60-80% ROR
Series A Funds	40-60% ROR
Series B Funds	20-30% ROR

Remember, these numbers (and those that follow) are highly generalized so as to be illustrative. They will vary greatly depending on many factors relating specifically to your company, market, and investors (including, but not limited to, whether you're talking to a strategic or non-strategic investor, level of rapport established, and the investor's affinity for the market). However, these conservative numbers can be used as guidelines to give you a basic idea of what to expect in each round.

Why is it the case that a Series B Fund will expect a smaller rate of return than a seed fund? On top of the amount of risk, investors will factor in Principle #2 – Hold Times.

PRINCIPLE 2 - TIME IS YOUR ENEMY

Hold times play a large role in determining how much equity an investor will want for their investment (review *Table 4.2*). Investors put you "on the clock" the minute they invest money in your startup...the longer they believe it will take to harvest your company, the more equity they'll need to own to achieve their required rate of return.

hold times
the time between the date of the purchase of an asset and the date of the sale of the asset

It typically takes most startups 7-10 years to reach a liquidity event (such as an acquisition or IPO). Investors usually project their investments and valuations based on the following hold times (*Table 4.3*):

Average Hold Times	
Angel / Seed Funds	8-10 years
Series A Funds	5-7 years
Series B Funds	3-5 years

Minimizing these hold times is of great value to you as the founder. It is important for you to build as much of your business as possible without raising equity capital, because if investors perceive that it will take longer to harvest the business, they'll require more equity. This will lower the overall valuation of your company when raising initial capital – something you want to guard against as much as possible.

The best way to illustrate this is through an example.

EXAMPLE 4.1

Amy, a seed-stage investor, wants to invest $500,000 in MealNow. After identifying all of the risks, Amy decides that she needs a 75% ROR to make her investment worthwhile. Amy believes that if Sara executes well on MealNow's plan, the company has the potential to get acquired for $100MM within 7-8 years.

How much equity does Amy need for this investment, and how does it affect valuation?

First, determine the capital that will be returned to Amy, using this formula:

$$\text{Amount Invested} \ \times \ (1 + \text{ROR})^{\text{\# of Years Held}}$$

Situation 1, holding 7 years: $500,000 \times (1 + .75)^7 =$ **$25,132,537.84**
Situation 2, holding 8 years: $500,000 \times (1 + .75)^8 =$ **$43,981,941.22**

Next, determine the equity Amy should receive for her investment:

$$\text{Ownership \%} = \text{Capital Returned} / \text{Anticipated Exit}$$

Situation 1, holding 7 years: $25,132,537 / $100,000,000 = **25.13%**
Situation 2, holding 8 years: $43,981,941 / $100,000,000 = **43.98%**

Finally, determine the post-money valuation of MealNow, using this formula:

$$\text{PMV} = \text{Amount Invested} / \text{Equity Received for Investment}$$

Situation 1, holding 7 years: $500,000 / .2513 = **$1,989,653.80**
Situation 2, holding 8 years: $500,000 / .4398 = **$1,136,880.40**

Plug the values into the following table to compare the effects of holding times:

Investment	ROR	# Years to Exit	Capital Returned to Amy	Anticipated Exit	Equity Amy Needs to Hit ROR	PMV of MealNow
$500,000	75%	7	$25,132,537.84	$100,000,000	25.13%	$1,989,653.80
$500,000	75%	8	$43,981,941.22	$100,000,000	43.98%	$1,136,880.40

As you can see, the difference of just one year almost doubles the equity that Amy needs to realize her ROR, and reduces MealNow's overall post-money valuation by close to $800,000.

It's clear that time horizons play a huge factor in how a business is valued by an investor – bootstrap as much as you can early on to build value before investors come in. That way, you'll be one step closer to a successful exit and can hold onto more equity while boosting the valuation of your company.

PRINCIPLE 3 - CAST THE VISION

At its core, startup investing is nothing more than buying stock at a negotiated price today so you can sell it for a higher price at some point in the future. The only way to drive up valuation of a company in the early stages is to convince investors that they will be able to do just that. You must be able to sell investors on the belief that both the timing and the product are right, as well as the belief that you have put together the best team to execute on it. If you can't cast the vision – create a compelling story – that your company can sell stock at a future price that is 50-100x's what it is worth today, it will be hard to justify a high valuation.

future value
the sum to which today's investment will grow by a specific future date when compounded at a given interest rate

While there needs to be some compelling evidence to validate assertions of market opportunity for your scalable product, the burden of demonstrating **future value** is squarely on the shoulders of the founding team.

scale
if gaining additional revenue requires relatively smaller and smaller additions of operating costs, your business is scalable

How do you demonstrate that both the market and the timing are right (using hard evidence outside of the softer storytelling skills)? Let's look at an example:

EXAMPLE 4.2

It's 2001 and George wants to start a business to help other companies launch websites. He bootstraps his operations for a while and helps a few dozen companies launch websites that their customers love. Now, he wants to raise $5 million to help more companies transition to the web.

To demonstrate to investors that his company could be worth $1 billion, he points to estimates by credible research firms saying that the number of business websites will grow from 36 million in 2001 to over 186 million in 2008.[viii]

While George and his investors know that he alone will not be responsible for that level of growth, it is clear that the market is ripe with opportunity and that it is big enough to support several "winners."

Although the company will not be scalable if George himself (or a team of workers) has to build a unique website for each customer, George can pivot the company into building a platform in which any business could instantly create their own customized website. This would give the product the ability to efficiently scale with the market.

As described in the example above, in addition to a massive market opportunity, you will need to demonstrate that the product or service can **scale** with the market. One way to do this is through a **platform business**. Platform businesses are infinitely more attractive to investors, as they have the potential to reach more people and therefore throw off more returns.

platform business
businesses that allow users to create and consume value, i.e. users (producers) can create value on the platform for other users (consumers) to consume. Ex: Facebook, Twitter, YouTube, and Google

Regardless of whether you've built a platform business or something else entirely, convincingly painting the picture of why your product is right for a specific market at a specific time will help to increase your company's valuation.

Learning how to effectively cast the vision for your company is more than just learning how to tell a story, though. For that reason, it is a practice full of nuances and methodologies that are outside the scope of this book. We introduce the importance of it here because it plays a critical role within the capital raising process. How well or poorly you are able to communicate your vision for the company will have a night and day impact on the terms you're able to negotiate. Because of that, it is truly one of the most important things you can do in order to successfully raise money! We recommend consulting additional resources to build proficiency in this area.[ix]

PRINCIPLE 4 - FUTURE CAPITAL RAISES AFFECT VALUATION

In addition to risk and time, subsequent capital raises affect your startup's valuation. Remember the concept of dilution? If you revisit Chapter 2, you'll notice that each time you raise equity capital for your company, the existing equity holders' percentage of ownership goes down.

retention ratio
a backend calculation that helps to determine how much equity to request

Although dilution is a normal part of the process (and there can be both good and bad dilution, as we've discussed), investors establish their ROR with the expectation that they will own the negotiated amount of equity through the exit. To protect themselves against dilution from future raises, investors drive down the valuation by applying a **retention ratio**.

Let's look at Sara's negotiations with Amy to see how retention ratios affect valuation:

EXAMPLE 4.3

Amy has determined that her fund needs 25% ownership of MealNow in exchange for a $500,000 investment, giving MealNow a post-money valuation of $2 million (remember, post-money valuation is $500,000 / 25%). However, Amy thinks that Sara will need to raise an additional $10 million over the next five years to reach the potential $100 million exit.

In order to raise the next $10 million, Amy thinks that Sara will have to sell 50% of the equity. If this is true, Amy will only own 12.5% of the company upon exit…half of what she needs to reach her required ROR. To protect her fund from this situation, Amy applies a retention ratio to her valuation negotiations.

To figure out the percentage of equity she needs today to secure 25% equity upon exit, she uses the retention ratio formula:

$$\text{Equity Needed (based on retention ratio)} = \frac{\% \text{ Ownership Needed at Exit}}{(1 - \text{Expected Future \% Equity Sold})}$$

Apply the retention ratio formula to Amy's situation:

$$\text{Equity Needed} = \frac{25\%}{(1 - .5)} = 50\%$$

As you can see, Amy's calculation shows that she needs 50% of MealNow's equity today, knowing that her position will be diluted down to 25% by the time the company has an exit.

EXAMPLE 4.3 CONT.

How does this change in equity required by Amy affect MealNow's valuation? (Remember, use the post-money valuation formula for *Example 4.1*)

$$\$500,000 \ / \ .5 \ = \ \mathbf{\$1,000,000}$$

The ratio clearly has a huge affect on Sara. Instead of a $2 million post-money valuation from Amy's investment, MealNow falls to a post-money valuation of $1 million.

Retention ratios are a common safeguard used by investors to lower your valuation and get the equity they require. While raising multiple rounds of capital may be necessary, it is important to be cognizant of the ways in which it can affect your present valuation.

PRINCIPLE 5 - THE EMPLOYEE OPTION POOL

The final factor affecting valuation is the employee option pool. Although all investors want to see equity reserved for employees – to incentivize employees to build a highly valued company quickly – they may attempt to bake the option pool into the pre-money valuation. This ends up lowering the valuation for the founders and early investors by lowering the **price per share**.

price per share determines how many shares an investor can buy for a given dollar investment

EXAMPLE 4.4

Suppose you are able to negotiate a $1,000,000 investment on a $4,000,000 pre-money valuation. If there are 2,000,000 outstanding shares amongst the founders and early investors, this should mean the investor would acquire shares at a price of $2.00 per share. However, if the investor wants to create a 10% option pool before his investment *and* include the value of the option pool in the pre-money valuation, the share price will end up being lower than $2.00. Here's how:

Step 1: Find the number of shares issued for the option pool (revisit *Example 2.1* if you need to review the formula).

$$\text{New Equity Pool} \ = \ \frac{2,000,000}{(1 - .10)} \ - \ 2,000,000 \ = \ 222,222 \text{ shares}$$

Step 2: Calculate the revised share price with the option pool included in the total pool of shares.

$$\frac{\$4,000,000}{2,000,000 \text{ shares} + 222,222 \text{ options}} \ = \ \$1.80 \text{ per share}$$

You can see that the option pool is combined with the total outstanding shares, which is then divided into the pre-money valuation to find the share price. Adding the option pool into this mix lowers price per share from $2.00 to $1.80. The net effect is that the investor will be able to acquire more shares of the company at the lower share price than at the higher price for the same amount of total money invested.

To avoid this artificial lowering of the share price, negotiate the pre-money valuation without an option pool to determine the agreed upon share price. Then create the option pool and take in the investment at that negotiated share price.

4.2 THE VENTURE GAME™ VALUATION MODEL

Reconciling all of the above principles can be confusing. That's why we created *The Venture Game™ Valuation Model* - it's a simple valuation model for startups that combines theories used in the **First Chicago Method of Valuation** and the **Terminal Value Method of Valuation**. It also considers the creation of the employee option pool to give you (and investors) a tool to utilize when determining a valuation for and the share price of a startup for purposes of an investment.

Let's first break down the pieces of The Venture Game™ Valuation Model:

> The First Chicago Method of Valuation takes into account the probability of various outcomes for the business, ranging from a complete failure to a huge exit. In other words, it looks at the business in terms of best case, worst case, and most likely scenarios.[x]

> The Terminal Value Method of Valuation (also called the Venture Capital Method), discounts the expected future value of the company to a present value based on an investor's ROR. Additionally, the model accounts for the dilution that is expected to occur when the company raises additional equity capital in the future.[xi]

Although they are widely used models, they both leave out several factors. As such, we combine them with considerations on an employee option pool to encompass all of the five principles discussed. This valuation tool is designed to boil an investment down to its actual share price so you can better determine how many shares you must issue an investor.

There are several assumptions that must be outlined before you can fully build your valuation model. Remember, these are "guestimates" at best. However, if you can agree on the assumptions with potential investors, you'll arrive at a valuation that makes sense for the business. To fill in the parts of the model not covered by the assumptions, you'll need to go through a series of calculations utilizing the formulas on the following page.

ASSUMPTIONS TO MAKE FOR THE VENTURE GAME™ VALUATION MODEL:

- Best, middle, and worst-case scenarios for company (exit value)
- Probability of each of the three scenarios occurring
- Estimated number of years investment is held
- Investor's ROR requirement (based on risk and time)
- Expected future dilution of the company (in order to reach best case scenario)
- Size of investment

FORMULAS FOR THE VENTURE GAME™ VALUATION MODEL:

Present Value

$$\frac{\text{Exit Value}}{(1 + \text{ROR})^{\text{\# Years Investment is Held}}}$$

Revised Present Value

Present Value of Scenario x Probability of Occurence

Estimated Present Value

Add 3 "Revised Present Values" together

Ownership Requirement at Exit

$$\frac{\text{Investment Size}}{\text{Estimated Present Value}}$$

Revised Equity Ownership

$$\frac{\text{Ownership Req. at Exit}}{1 - \text{Future Dilution}}$$

Post-Money Valuation

$$\frac{\text{Investment}}{\text{Revised Equity Ownership}}$$

Pre-Money Valuation

Post-Money Valuation - Size of Investment

Share Price (before Option Pool)

$$\frac{\text{Pre-Money Valuation}}{\text{Total Shares before Option Pool}}$$

Revised Shares (after Option Pool)

$$\frac{\text{Total Shares}}{1 - \text{Option Pool \%}}$$

Revised Price Per Share (after Option Pool)

$$\frac{\text{Pre-Money Valuation}}{\text{Total Shares after Option Pool}}$$

SPREADSHEET STRUCTURE FOR THE VENTURE GAME™ VALUATION MODEL:

	Best Case	Middle Case	Worst Case
Exit Type	IPO	Acquisition	Liquidation
Exit Value			
ROR			
# Years Investment Held			
Present Value			
Probability of Occurrence			
Revised Present Value			

Estimated Present Value	
Size of Investment	
Ownership Requirement @ Exit	
Expected Future Dilution	
Revised Equity Ownership	
Post Money Valuation	
Pre Money Valuation	
Outstanding Shares (before Option Pool)	
Price Per Share (before Option Pool)	
New Option Pool	
Shares after Creating Option Pool	
Price Per Share (after Option Pool)	
New Shares Issued to Investor	

Let's look at an example of valuing a startup to see how the model works.

EXAMPLE 4.5

Amy and Sara are in the midst of negotiations to complete a $500,000 investment in Meal-Now. However, they haven't yet settled on a valuation. To think through all the variables, Amy is going to use The Venture Game™ Valuation Model. She comes up with the following assumptions:

	Best Case	Middle Case	Worst Case
Exit Type	IPO	Acquisition	Liquidation
Exit Value	$2,000,000,000	$75,000,000	$5,000,000
ROR	70%	70%	70%
# Years Investment Held	7	7	7
Present Value			
Probability of Occurrence	5%	35%	60%
Revised Present Value			

Amy knows that there are 1,000,000 outstanding shares of MealNow. She expects that there will be a future dilution of 60% and a 10% option pool created.

EXAMPLE 4.5 CONT.

Amy uses the formulas to complete the model and ends up with the following table:

	Best Case	Middle Case	Worst Case
Exit Type	IPO	Acquisition	Liquidation
Exit Value	$2,000,000,000	$75,000,000	$5,000,000
ROR	70%	70%	70%
# Years Investment Held	7	7	7
Present Value	$48,740,227	$1,827,759	$121,851
Probability of Occurrence	5%	35%	60%
Revised Present Value	$2,437,011.34	$639,715.48	$73,110.34

Estimated Present Value	$3,149,837.16
Size of Investment	$500,000
Ownership Requirement @ Exit	15.87%
Expected Future Dilution	60%
Revised Equity Ownership	39.68%
Post Money Valuation	$1,259,934.86
Pre Money Valuation	$759,934.86
Outstanding Shares (before Option Pool)	1,000,000
Price Per Share (before Option Pool)	$0.76
New Option Pool	10%
Shares after Creating Option Pool	1,111,111
Price Per Share (after Option Pool)	$0.68
New Shares Issued to Investor	735,294

By going through these calculations, Amy has accounted for every possible factor that can affect valuation, including:

- Various scenarios and probabilities
- Future dilution due to subsequent capital raises
- The amount of time it will take to get capital returned
- An option pool created before she invests (and what will happen if it is created after she invests)

From the model, we can see that taking the best, middle, and worst case scenarios into account, MealNow is currently valued at $3,149,837.16 (the estimated present value in the table above). This valuation - combined with the other factors listed above - will help guide Sara and Amy in reaching an agreement in their funding negotiations.

What about companies that are not destined for a big exit?

Some businesses (even profitable ones) can struggle to raise equity capital from investors who are seeking big returns. Here, the math of valuations works against the startup.

EXAMPLE 4.6

Imagine that, instead of the assumptions used in *Example 4.5*, Amy comes up with the following assumptions for MealNow:

	Best Case	Middle Case	Worst Case
Exit Type	IPO	Acquisition	Liquidation
Exit Value	$100,000,000	$25,000,000	$5,000,000
ROR	70%	70%	70%
# Years Investment Held	7	7	7
Present Value			
Probability of Occurrence	5%	35%	60%
Revised Present Value			

After a few quick calculations, we can see that an investment in the startup doesn't make sense:

	Best Case	Middle Case	Worst Case
Exit Type	IPO	Acquisition	Liquidation
Exit Value	$100,000,000	$25,000,000	$5,000,000
ROR	70%	70%	70%
# Years Investment Held	7	7	7
Present Value	$2,437,011.34	$609,252.83	$121,850.57
Probability of Occurrence	5%	35%	60%
Revised Present Value	$121,850.57	$213,238.49	$73,110.34

Estimated Present Value	$408,199.40
Size of Investment	$500,000

Assuming the same holding times and required ROR, Amy would have to own 100% of the company in order to confidently make a $500,000 investment.

However, without a meaningful equity stake, Sara will not be incentivized to go through the trials and tribulations all founders face when building their first company.

As such, an investment in this scenario would not be feasible.

Coming up with a valuation is more of an art than science. By understanding all of the factors that investors consider, you will have a better sense of the value of your company at different stages of the capital formation process. Use this to your advantage, and keep thinking bigger!

Remember, the purpose of this isn't to create as many complex spreadsheets for each area of the business as you can. That is a waste of time. These models are meant to serve as a quick guide to help you figure out appropriate investment levels and valuation ranges for your company.

KEY TAKEAWAYS

- Investors judge the risks your startup faces and use those perceived factors to calculate the return they need to achieve in order to make an investment in your company worthwhile.

- Bootstrap and build as much as possible before seeking equity investments – time horizons can dictate how much your company is worth and how much you have to pay out.

- Investors will work to protect themselves against the creation of option pools and future capital raises. These actions can impact your valuation!

CHAPTER 5
NEGOTIATING EQUITY INVESTMENTS

Up to this point, things have gone well for MealNow. After spending time conducting diligence on potential investors and landing on what they believe is an appropriate valuation for the company, several qualified investors have expressed their interest to Sara and Mike.

However, they now realize that valuation is just the beginning of the negotiations!

Through talking with other entrepreneur friends who have gone through the capital-raising process, Mike and Sara have learned there are certain deal terms investors will request before investing in the company.

Mike and Sara want to have a strong position going into the negotiations – in order to meet their own needs as well as satisfy those of the investors – so they enlist the help of their friends in order to better understand the investor mindset.

5.1 UNDERSTANDING BOTH SIDES OF THE TABLE

In addition to knowing what goes into an equity investment from the valuation perspective, it is also critical to understand the individuals and groups you are negotiating with. As we previously mentioned, getting a better idea of their histories, experiences, and beliefs (about things like the market, investment strategies, dynamics with portfolio companies and founders, among others) will help you understand what drives their negotiations. If you go in with a general idea of what they'll be looking to gain or terms they might not budge on, you'll be better able to address those issues before (or when) they arise.

You must also examine your own motivations…what YOU want and expect to get out of the negotiations. Are those things reasonable?

To you, they may seem so. Now, look at them from the perspective of the investor. Do they still seem reasonable? If so, and if you have an idea of what to expect from the investing groups, there is a good chance that both sides will be able to come to an agreement that is generally satisfactory for both parties.

In the next two sections, we list some of the common needs and concerns that investors have, as well as some reasonable expectations that you, as a founder, should have for investors.

5.2 MEETING INVESTORS' NEEDS - WHAT DO THEY WANT?

Investors will enter negotiations expecting some level of upside to (or, at least, protection from) taking on risk in your company. These needs may include:

A LEVEL OF REWARD COMMISERATE WITH THE LEVEL OF RISK This may seem obvious. In fact, we've discussed it before. Revisit Chapter 4 and you'll remember that coming up with a required rate of return is a pretty subjective estimate by the investor, based on the level of risk they perceive they are taking on. However, it generally follows that the earlier the investment, the greater the chance of failure. Thus, early investors take on more risk and therefore demand a greater return. If you aren't comfortable with having to reward early investors with a high ROR, you have another option: bootstrap the company as much as you possibly can. Hold off on raising money until you absolutely need it to get the business to the next level of growth.

SUFFICIENT INFLUENCE ON THE DEVELOPMENT OF THE COMPANY Investors who have an applicable base of experience will want to work with you to accelerate the speed of an investment return. They can help drive development in a variety of ways: through giving input on the key strategic decisions that set the trajectory of the company early on, by mentoring the founding and managing teams, or by networking with other potential investors (as well as future customers or strategic partners). These types of qualified and engaged investors – the investors that you want to seek out – will pass on opportunities to invest if they feel that the founding team is only interested in their capital. These investors have a psychological need to be involved in the development of the company, so it is in your best interest to find the investors whose experience aligns with the company's trajectory.

MINIMIZED TAXES RELATIVE TO THE STRUCTURE OF THE COMPANY Different types of investors prefer various company structures for write-off and taxing purposes. Smaller-scale, more involved angel investors typically prefer to invest in a **pass-through** entity. This gives them the ability to write off the investments made during the early stages of the company. However, VCs with investments in multiple companies prefer that the company is set up as a **C-Corp**, as it bypasses the administrative hassles of a pass-through entity.

pass-through
a firm's owners pay income tax on the firm's income and not the firm

What administrative hassles, you ask? Pass-through entities must issue a K1 return to each investor for each tax year, meaning that institutional investors cannot file their business tax returns until they receive a K1 from each startup they've invested in. As you may guess, startups are notorious for not filing their tax returns on time…which can cause real headaches for an investor that holds a portfolio of 10-20 investments.

c-corp
business that is a completely separate tax entity from its owners (unlike a partnership)

LIQUIDATION PREFERENCE OVER PREVIOUS INVESTORS AND FOUNDERS A standard rule in startup investing is "last money in, first money out," meaning that upon a liquidation event, the last people to invest will get paid before previous investors and the founders. Investors will also want to obtain preferred shares of equity with a return preference. These stipulations ensure that if the company achieves an exit that falls short of everyone's expectations, the investor(s) will get their payout(s) before the common equity gets any of the proceeds. We'll discuss these various types of equity more in-depth in Chapter 6.

LIQUIDITY, WHETHER THE BUSINESS IS SUCCESSFUL OR NOT Investors always look for the exit. They're also on a short (and pressured) time frame in terms of tying up their money in your company. Investors see little to no benefit in holding capital in a company that is clearly not going to materialize into a huge exit, so they add provisions that allow them to exit the business within a reasonable window of time (typically 5-7 years). Such provisions could mean that the investor reserves the right to force the sale of the business, even though you may not want to sell. Such provisions could also mean that you as the founder have to "cash out" the investor by redeeming her shares (see page 82 for more information on this topic).

VOTING CONTROL WHEN PERFORMANCE IS BELOW EXPECTATIONS Short and sweet: savvy investors will want to have the power to make changes to the company's management if the founding team is underperforming and the business is not growing at the rate investors believe it could be. It is, however, unreasonable for investors to demand control when things are going well and the founding team is driving performance in line with expectations.

THE NEED TO BUILD A REPUTATION An often-overlooked component of the deal-making process is that investors want and need to exit a deal with their reputation in tact (or even strengthened). If they screw you over – whether intentionally or otherwise – it will shape future entrepreneurs' perceptions of them and ultimately impact the quality of deal flow that comes their way. In an age of increasing connectedness - especially in the entrepreneurial and investing communities where personal recommendations and introductions reign supreme - the need to create positive, lasting relationships with founders of portfolio companies is becoming more and more important to investors. Long-term investors understand this and will try to be as fair as possible, while at the same time negotiating deals that address their main concerns.

5.3 MEETING YOUR NEEDS AS A FOUNDER

As a founder, there is a set of reasonable expectations you can hold when going into investor negotiations. Most practiced investors will understand this and will work to meet those needs. As long as you aren't unreasonable in your demands, most of the following needs can be met:

ABILITY TO LEAD THE CREATION OF THE BUSINESS YOU CONCEPTUALIZED Paul Graham, co-founder of Y Combinator, has said that investors should realize that passion drives determination, and determination (more so than intelligence) drives performance. It's not unreasonable for you to expect to play a role in leading the company. You also have the right to expect a little forgiveness when you make a few mistakes – it's a natural part of the startup process, especially if this is your first company. However, be aware that investors won't be willing to give you multiple re-do's as mistakes compile.

FINANCIAL REWARD FOR CREATING AND MANAGING THE BUSINESS Just as investors require a sufficient return on their capital, founders need a sufficient return on time and talent. Savvy investors are extremely concerned about ensuring that those building the company be handsomely compensated in the way of stock options. This plays in your favor, as long as you are one of those that builds the company!

ADEQUATE RESOURCES TO BUILD THE COMPANY You'll need an appropriate amount of runway to prove out your business model, acquire customers, and get to commercialization. The length of time and capital required varies based on the type of deal and stage of development the company is in, but it is not unreasonable for you to ask for around 18 months of runway to drive the business to the next logical stage.

MEANINGFUL CONTRIBUTIONS FROM INVESTORS It has been said that money doesn't build companies, people do. Money is the means to an end, the "gas in the tank," if you will. When bringing money into the company, you should fully understand the investor's commitment with respect to networking, bringing in potential customers and all-star talent, and introducing you to future investors. You want (and should expect) investors to bring value into the company over and above their capital investment.

ABILITY TO BUILD A REPUTATION It's very likely that you will raise capital multiple times throughout your career, whether that is through several rounds with your current company or whether you become a serial entrepreneur. If you build a reputation now for being unreasonable with investors, you'll be surprised at how quickly word travels within the investing community and just how much harder it will become to obtain equity financing in the future. Make it your goal to come out of each deal with a reputation and relationships that can serve you well in future deals.

5.4 WE ALL WANT THE SAME THING

There are several areas in which founders and investors typically see eye to eye in terms of what they expect in a deal. Here are a couple of examples:

FLEXIBILITY OF STRUCTURE THAT ALLOWS FOR FOLLOW-ON INVESTMENTS Avoid complex investment structures at all costs – they are not attractive to subsequent investors. If both parties want to give the business the best chance to succeed (and why wouldn't they?), you'll find a way to keep the structures simple…especially early in the company's life.

dead equity
equity held by
employees and
founders no longer
working at the
startup

ELIMINATE THE POTENTIAL FOR "DEAD EQUITY" Neither party wants to see key team members with a sizeable chunk of equity walk away from the company prematurely to pursue other opportunities. Nothing is more demoralizing than watching an absentee, non-investing owner get rich off the backs of those building the company.

INCENTIVES FOR MANAGEMENT While both sides typically see the benefit in allocating an appropriate amount of equity to an option pool in order to recruit and retain all-star management team members, you might not necessarily agree on how it is done. The big question up for discussion: do the investors or founders get diluted to make this happen? Often, the outcome will depend on who has made concessions in other areas during the negotiations.

5.5 THE BIG 3: ESSENTIAL TERMS FOR EVERY DEAL

In the end, there are three terms that are present in virtually every venture deal. VC's will require rights that cover every scenario is some way. Brad Feld puts this belief succinctly by saying that VC's need rights for "up, down, and to know what the f*** is going on."[xii]

UP: Investors want the opportunity to stay engaged when things are going well for the company. Rights to pro-rata participation in future rounds - allowing them to maintain their ownership - protect them in "up scenarios.

DOWN: Investors want to recoup their money as easily (and painlessly) as possible if things don't go so well for the company. Liquidation preferences and redemption rights allow them to collect their money first when things are "down" and they want to exit.

KNOW WHAT'S GOING ON: Investors want some sort of control in…or at least knowledge of…decisions that are being made and things that are happening within the startup. Giving large-scale investors the right to a seat on the Board of Directors will enable them to be "in the know" as much as possible without actually being in the weeds of building the business.

We will go into further detail on each specific term in the coming pages. However, it is important for you to understand that while the specifics of each of these provisions can be negotiated, they are likely to be the three core terms in any equity investment agreement you enter.

Although each section in this chapter is not exhaustive, it should give you a good idea of how to approach this phase of investor negotiations. Not only will you have a better idea of some of the things they may ask for or require in order to invest in your company, but you'll also have a strong position to work from in satisfying your own needs.

KEY TAKEAWAYS

- There are multiple stages to investor negotiations. Before going in, you must not only have a clear and compelling picture of what you're asking for and why, but you must also study the investors to best anticipate what position they may take as well.

- Be prepared: there is a good chance that you will have to make concessions in areas you didn't think you would have to. But remember, this is what negotiations are all about.

- There are some areas where investors and founders typically agree. Use those areas to build goodwill with your investors in order to give yourself a better shot at fulfilling your other needs.

CHAPTER 6
EQUITY CLASS PAYOUTS:
STAYING AFLOAT UNDER THE WATERFALL

The nuances of deal terms discussed during investor negotiations will play a large role in dictating how much of a payout each equity holder actually receives upon a liquidation event in the company.

This is the truly high-stakes part of negotiations, and Mike and Sara have to be careful – if they don't fully understand what certain investment terms mean, it is likely that they'll only receive a fraction of what they expect upon payout.

So, what do you, as a founder, need to keep an eye out for? Let's join Mike and Sara as they navigate various equity class characteristics.

6.1 TYPES OF EQUITY - AN OVERVIEW

Valuation is only one piece the puzzle when it comes to an equity investment. In Chapter 2, we talked about issuing new pools of equity each time you raise a round of funding. When it comes to the more "institutional" investors (aka not your friends and family), you can expect to issue a new **class** of equity in addition to a new pool.

What we mean here is that not only is the ownership relegated to a new pool (to separate it out from the other investments previously made in order to determine share price and amount of shares purchased in each round), but it is also a different *type* of ownership. Investor equity classes will have different attributes and rights than founder's equity, typically allowing investors to receive their payouts first and, many times, at higher percentages than what they actually own.

This may seem unfair, but in the startup world, the rule of thumb is that money always gets paid back before time and talent receive a cut.

Let's look at a quick example to see how and why this works:

class of equity
types of equity that have different attributes, characteristics, or payoff benefits

EXAMPLE 6.1

Suppose Sara raises $250,000 from Angel Bill in exchange for 25% of the common equity (common equity is the same equity class as founder's shares). A day later, Sara decides to pay a one-time $200,000 dividend to the common shareholders. From this payout, Angel Bill receives $50,000 (equivalent to 25% of the payout, in line with his ownership percentage) and Sara receives $150,000 (75% of the payout, equivalent to her ownership percentage).

This is just an illustrative example, as founders would likely not (or should not) make such an obviously poor decision as using investor money to pay shareholders rather than to build the business.

Like any investor, Angel Bill wants to protect his $250,000 investment. If, instead of owning common equity, Angel Bill held preferred class equity, he could prevent this situation. With preferred class, Angel Bill is entitled to having his $250,000 re-paid before any pro-rata distributions are paid to the common shareholders...meaning he would receive the entire $200,000 dividend.

As you can see from the example, different classes of equity have drastically different distribution outcomes. While there are multiple types of equity classes that can be issued to investor, the two most common types are **preferred shares** (also known as convertible preferred shares) and participating preferred shares.

preferred shares
dividends are paid before anything is paid to common stock holders in the event of a liquidation

6.2 PREFERRED SHARES (AKA CONVERTIBLE PREFERRED SHARES)

The main advantage of this form of equity is that it provides for the repayment of the invested capital at a **return preference** plus a negotiated **accrued dividend** upon a liquidity event. As noted, the invested capital and accrued dividends are paid out in full before the common

return preference
often listed in multiples of the original investment amount

accrued dividends
dividend that is considered to be earned but not declared or payable

shareholders receive any payout on their equity.

Where does the "convertible" come from, you ask? Well, with this form of equity, the investor has two options upon a liquidity event:

- The investor can exercise his preferred shares as previously described and receive his initial investment plus accrued dividends upon payout.
- Conversely, the investor has the option to receive the accrued dividends and convert his ownership into the underlying common stock at a pre-determined valuation, enabling him to stay protected on the downside (via dividends) but capture some of the upside (via a conversion into common equity).

Reading that can be confusing. Let's see convertible preferred shares in action:

EXAMPLE 6.2

This time, suppose that Sara raises $250,000 from Angel Bill in exchange for 250,000 convertible preferred shares with a 1x return preference (equivalent to 25% of the company.)

Bill can exercise the option to convert the convertible preferred shares into common shares on a 1 to 1 basis, meaning that he has the option to convert each preferred share owned into one share of common equity.

Sara does not raise any more equity capital, but in five years, she sells the company to a competitor for $5 million.

What does Angel Bill receive at liquidation?

If Bill does not convert his preferred shares into common shares, his return preference dictates that he gets a payout of **$250,000** – his original investment.

If, however, Bill exercises his option to convert the preferred shares into common shares, he receives a payout equivalent to his ownership percentage, 25% of the company.

$$.25 \times \$5,000,000 = \mathbf{\$1,250,000}$$

In this instance, it's obvious that Bill will choose to convert his convertible preferred shares into common shares, because he stands to make more money on the deal as a common shareholder.

EXAMPLE 6.3

What if MealNow is struggling, and Sara is forced to sell to a competitor for $350,000 in cash?

If Bill does not convert his shares into common shares, he receives his return preference as a payout: **$250,000**. Although he didn't make anything on the deal, he didn't lose anything, either.

EXAMPLE 6.3 CONT.

If Bill exercises his option to convert the convertible preferred shares into common shares, he will receive 25% of the company's value (commiserate with his percentage ownership of the company):

$$.25 \times \$350,000 = \textbf{\$87,500}$$

In *Example 6.3*, it is not in Angel Bill's interest to convert his convertible preferred shares into common shares…he would lose money instead of recouping his initial investment.

With convertible preferred shares, there is a reasonable balance between risk and reward for both the founders and investors. It's a protective measure for investors, in that it gives them a good chance of recovering their investment at the very least, coupled with the benefit of a high upside if things work out well for the company.

However, some investors view this structure as being too favorable for founders and instead pursue participating preferred shares.

6.3 PARTICIPATING PREFERRED SHARES

Participating preferred shares give the investor the best of both worlds: instead of having to choose between receiving only their return preference or converting into common shares, participating preferred shares allow them to receive both.

This form of equity provides for the repayment of the invested capital (at the return preference) before the common shareholders receive any payout on their equity. In addition, the shares come with the right to participate as a common shareholder in the exit.

participating preferred shares shareholders' payouts include the initial amount invested, dividends, and a conversion into common stock

EXAMPLE 6.4

Sara raises $250,000 from Angel Bill in exchange for 250,000 participating preferred shares at a 1x return preference (equivalent to 25% of the company). Sara does not raise any more equity capital, but in five years, she sells the company to a competitor for $5 million. What does Angel Bill receive at liquidation?

Step 1: Find the amount Bill receives based on return preference.

Amount Invested x Return Preference
$250,000 x 1 = $250,000

Step 2: Find Bill's payout as a common shareholder when he converts into common shares.

(Buyout Price – Return Preference) x % Ownership

($5,000,000 - $250,000) x 25% = $1,187,500

EXAMPLE 6.4 CONT.

Bill doesn't have to choose between these two payouts…he gets both! As such, the total that Bill receives upon exit is:

$$\$250,000 + \$1,187,500 = \$1,437,500$$

As you can see, Angel Bill makes more money if his ownership is in participating preferred shares as opposed to convertible preferred shares.

EXAMPLE 6.5

What if Sara is forced to sell Meal Now for $350,000? Follow the same process to find Bill's payout.

Step 1: Find Bill's return preference payout.

$$\$250,000 \text{ x } 1 = \$250,000$$

Step 2: Find Bill's payout as a common shareholder when he converts into common shares.

$$(\$350,000 - \$250,000) \text{ x } 25\% = \$25,000$$

Step 3: Find Bill's total payout.

$$\$250,000 + \$25,000 = \$275,000$$

In this instance, Bill gets a payout of nearly 80% of the total cash paid for Sara's company, even though he owned only 25% of the equity. You can now see why many investors prefer participating preferred shares, and why you have to carefully navigate these negotiations in order to protect your own equity payout!

6.4 CUMULATIVE DIVIDENDS

cumulative dividends
dividends that are an obligation regardless of the earnings of the company. Must be paid before any common stock dividends

Another payment type to be aware of is **cumulative dividends**. No matter what type of preferred shares you grant to an investor, you can expect that you'll have to pay the investor a dividend on their invested capital while you hold said capital.

Dividends typically range from 8-12% of invested capital per year. However, since startups are typically "cash starved" up to the point of exit, most dividends will accrue as a liability to be paid out upon the liquidity event.

EXAMPLE 6.6

Angel Bill invested $250,000 in MealNow and received preferred shares with a 10% cumulative dividend. Five years later, the company sells for $5,000,000. What will Bill receive in

EXAMPLE 6.6 CONT.

the form of cumulative dividends?

Investment x dividend % x number of years
$250,000 x 10% x 5 years = $125,000

Keep these dividends in mind, as they will be another required payout (on top of the returns from the investment itself) upon a company's exit.

6.5 THE WATERFALL

We hope it has become clear through the above examples that share options, return preferences, and cumulative dividends can account for a significant portion of the cash paid out upon liquidation, and that these factors play just as large of a role in your company as its valuation.

However, to fully understand the magnitude of the impact these shares can have on cash, let's calculate a **waterfall scenario**.

Note: Waterfall calculations can become incredibly complicated. For the purposes of this book, we show a very simplistic version of a waterfall scenario designed to help you understand some of the hurdles you may face.

waterfall scenario
specifies the order of distribution to investors upon a liquidity event

EXAMPLE 6.7

In the course of building MealNow, Sara raises three separate rounds of capital before she receives an offer to sell the business to a competitor for $25,000,000 in year 7.

Along with MealNow's cap table (below), consider that Angel Dave, Julie the VC, and Ben the VC each have participating preferred shares at a 1x or 2x return preference, and are to receive 10% cumulative dividends at the exit.

	Year 5	Year 4	Year 3	Year 2	Year 1	% Ownership
Round	Series B	Series A	Angel / Seed	F & F	Founders	% Ownership
Security Type	2x Participating	1x Participating	1x Participating	Common	Common	
Share Price	$11.15	$6.48	$3.11	$1.80	$0.02	
Mike					100,000	4.81%
Sara					500,000	24.05%
Parents				111,111		5.35%
Angel Dave			96,618			4.65%
VC Julie		770,751				37.08%
VC Ben	500,000					24.05%
Total Shares	500,000	770,751	96,618	111,111	600,000	2,078,480

EXAMPLE 6.7 CONT.

Based on the $25,000,000 buyout, let's breakdown the distribution of proceeds among the various parties:

Step 1: Calculate return preferences for each party.

Shares Owned x Share Price x Return Preference

Ben the VC = 500,000 x $11.15 x 2 = $11,150,000
Julie the VC = 770,751 x $6.48 x 1= $4,994,466
Angel Dave = 96,618 x $3.11 x 1= $300,482

Total = **$16,444,948**

Step 2: Calculate the cumulative dividends for each party.

Investment x Dividend % x Number of Years Held

Ben the VC = $5,575,000 x 10% x 3 = $1,672,500
Julie the VC = $4,994,466 x 10% x 4 = $1,997,787
Angel Dave = $300,482 x 10% x 5 = $150,241

Total = **$3,820,528**

Step 3: Calculate the proceeds to the common shareholders.

Buyout – Return Preferences – Cumulative Dividends = Proceeds to Common

$25MM - $16,444,948 - $3,820,528 = **$4,734,524**

Step 4: Determine the pro-rata distribution of common shares.

Common Ownership % x Proceeds to the Common

Mike (co-founder) = .0481 x $4,734,524 = $227,730
Sara (co-founder) = .2405 x $4,734,524 = $1,138,653
Parents = .0535 x $4,734,524 = $253,297
Angel Dave = .0465 x $4,734,524 = $220,155
Julie the VC = .3708 x $4,734,524 = $1,755,561
Ben the VC = .2405 x $4,734,524 = $1,138,653

Step 5: Create the payout schedule (next page).

As you can see, even though Sara owned 24.05% of the common shares, she only received 5.09% of the buyout price. The fact that Ben the VC was able to get a 2x liquidation preference on his participating preferred shares allowed him to receive 54% of the proceeds from the buyout, even though he only owned 24.08% of the common.

	Return Preference	Cumulative Dividends	Common Payout	Total	% of Buyout	Common Ownership
Mike			$ 227,730	$ 227,730	1.02%	4.81%
Sara			$ 1,138,653	$ 1,138,653	5.09%	24.05%
Parents			$ 253,297	$ 253,297	1.13%	5.35%
Angel Dave	$ 300,482	$ 150,241	$ 220,155	$ 670,878	2.79%	4.65%
VC Julie	$ 4,994,466	$ 1,997,787	$ 1,755,561	$ 8,747,814	35.82%	37.08%
VC Ben	$ 11,150,000	$ 1,672,500	$ 1,138,653	$ 13,961,153	54.15%	24.05%

Share types and conditions can be manipulated in such a way as to highly skew payouts in the investors' favor. Clearly, the type and structure of the equity is just as important as the valuation you receive for your company!

KEY TAKEAWAYS

- Various equity class types have different payout implications – know the difference between preferred shares (aka convertible preferred shares) and participating preferred shares.

- Be prepared to include cumulative dividends into your payout calculations – they add up and cannot be ignored!

- Structure your investment deals carefully; although you could own a significant portion of the common stock, your payout may not be commiserate with your level of ownership (or the work you put in) after stock types, preferences, and options are factored in.

CHAPTER 7
CALLING THE SHOTS

Throughout their capital-raising pursuits, Mike has become anxious about retaining control of the company. He tells Sara that they need to make sure that they cumulatively hold 51% of the company – bare minimum – to maintain control over the decisions made for MealNow's direction and operations.

Sara doesn't necessarily agree with him, though. Although she wants MealNow to maintain a certain amount of autonomy by not giving too much control to investing parties, she knows that it isn't all about percent ownership. There's a give-and-take aspect to it, she's sure, but she isn't fully aware of how it works.

So, how can Sara and Mike make sure that they have more control of the company's future than investors do? What factors give investors power over the company? Let's take a look.

Control in a company – especially a startup – is something of an illusion. It's something that everyone wants a piece of (or at the very least, understand)...but at the same time, it's something that shouldn't need "acted upon" until there's real trouble within the business. When things are going well, the management team should be able to rest easy – investors want to see more of the same. When things aren't going well, though, investors will want to see some changes made, and quick.

As stated earlier, when a person is an equity holder in a company, they care about the value of the company. It follows, then, that an equity-holding investor is going to want to have some sort of protective control over the direction of the company, no matter how small of a percentage they own in the company. They want to be sure the company increases in value over time.

Most investors are willing to provide enough space for a founding team to grow the business on their own...running multiple companies is not a scalable strategy for a VC. However, if things aren't going well within the business, investors will want to step in and assert some power. Because of this, certain control provisions are typically written into investment agreements.

7.1 BOARD RIGHTS

As has been discussed, the Board of Directors can play a large role in the overall direction of the company. You want strategic advisors on the board that not only have industry expertise and connections, but who will also mentor you and the business.

Oftentimes, a major or lead investor will require a seat on the board. They also may negotiate the ability to appoint other members to the board. For example, a lead investor may suggest a five-member board in which the founders appoint two members, the investor appoints two members, and both parties agree upon a fifth member.

This setup makes sense, because critical company decisions and discussions first occur at the board level. Additionally, boards typically meet quarterly, which allows investors to keep a pulse on the company's operational status.

The relationship between the board and the founding / managing team is one of the most important things you can manage in your startup. Because the board essentially has control over whether or not you remain head of the company during times of turmoil, you'll want them on your side.

As such, here are a few rules to live by when dealing with board members:

> **ERR ON THE SIDE OF TRANSPARENCY** Be open, honest, and factual with your information. They want company information, so give it to them! If you are open with them about the goings-on inside your startup, they will be more likely to get in the "problem-solving" mindset and help you see new strategies, opportunities, or solutions that you may be overlooking. If they consistently have to ask you for more data, that's not a good thing...make your communications with them more frequent and informative. Reaching out with updates more often than not is a

smart plan. Even if the investors don't always acknowledge or respond to the communication, they definitely pay attention and appreciate the transparency.

DON'T SURPRISE THE BOARD No board member should ever be surprised at a board meeting…do not wait until a board meeting to share bad news with them. Call each member before the meeting, making them aware of potentially negative situations. Nobody likes (negative) surprises, particularly investors.

COUNT THE VOTES BEFORE THE MEETING It's important to gather inputs and thoughts on certain key decisions – including budgets, new hires, etc. – well before the meeting. This not only gives you a stronger position to present from, but it also ensures that the board meetings serve as a smooth formality rather than as contentious platform for spirited discussions. It also helps set the agenda for meetings…and if something does need to get accomplished (i.e. you need advice or guidance on a key strategic decision), each board member will be better equipped to participate in and add value to the discussion.

If these rules seem simple or intuitive – good! There truly are no "tricks" to winning over the board. Be upfront, consistent, and timely with information. If you do just that, you shouldn't run into any serious problems.[1]

7.2 PROTECTIVE PROVISIONS

veto
the right to stop an action

Protective provisions give investors certain rights, such as **veto** power, over important decisions made by the founding team.

Key decisions investors will want at least partial control over include:

- C-level employee hirings
- Budgetary decisions (such as the right to approve or deny certain expenditures)
- Ability to liquidate the company
- Ability to raise additional equity capital
- Ability to issue additional equity to employees

Although protective provisions create more hurdles for founders to overcome while managing the company, founders still have the opportunity to "make their case" to investors to garner support for some of these key decisions.

1. It should go without stating that you should be running the business effectively as well! No amount of "goodwill" will overcome poor management decisions and sub-par operational outputs.

7.3 INFORMATION RIGHTS

Investors want to see their money being put to good use…in other words, producing returns. As such, many investors will require that they have the right to routinely obtain financial statements from the company.

Some will want to see monthly statements, while others will be fine with quarterly statements. Although this is an administrative hassle for startups, it is important to proactively provide the complete requested information on time. If you do so, you'll build goodwill with your investors, something that will come in handy down the road (whether it helps your current startup or a future venture). Remember Rule #1 of dealing with the board? That applies here, too.

Instead of looking at control provisions as restrictions on your ability to run the company, shift your paradigm to view these provisions as excellent opportunities to engage your investors and bring out their full commitment and support for your company.

Many entrepreneurs* mistakenly believe that if they hold at least 51% of the equity, they have complete control over the company. But none of the provisions above rely on a certain percentage of equity ownership in order to be acted upon. It's important to remember that here, control will come through outstanding performance and transparency...do as much as you can to execute on those two areas, and you'll set yourself up for success.

KEY TAKEAWAYS

- 51% founder ownership of the company is not indicative of complete ownership - investors will want control provisions written into investment agreements. These control provisions do not require a certain percent of equity to be held in order to be valid.

- Be transparent, timely, and complete in all of your dealings with the board and other investors to build goodwill.

- Control provisions can actually help you engage your investors to contribute to the company – use them to your advantage!

---

* This statement bears repeating: if you worry about maintaining complete control over the business, you should not raise money from investors. If you raise equity capital, you should be singularly driven to increase the overall valuation of the company, not maintain control over "your baby." Circumstances and performance should drive the decisions, not personal preferences.

CHAPTER 8
THE DREADED DOWN ROUND

Mike and Sara have heard of the dreaded down round; in fact, they've seen it happen to many of the startups around town during the last recession.

They know that, in order to best position the company for success, valuation must rise each time they raise a round of equity capital.

However, what happens if it doesn't? Is the company doomed? What happens to founder's equity, and what happens to the other investors? We'll discover the answers to these questions in the following pages.

8.1 DOWN ROUNDS - AN INTRODUCTION

Ideally, each time you raise capital you are able to tell a story of moving the business forward, as this helps your valuation to rise. However, this doesn't always happen in the real world: entrepreneurs are routinely faced with the prospect of raising capital at a valuation that is lower than what previous investors offered. This is called a down round, and you want to avoid it at all costs.

Down rounds occur for a variety of reasons, including:

MACRO FACTORS Sometimes, the economy plays a role in driving valuations down across the board (i.e. for all companies). If publicly traded companies' valuations are down (if they are trading at lower than normal values) due to a recession or some other comparable national / global event (such as the 2008 Debt Crisis), private company valuations will also be adversely affected.

PREVIOUS ROUND PRICED TOO HIGH Many times, first-time founders that raise an early stage round from family, friends, and unsophisticated investors set an artificially high valuation for their company...something that seems helpful at the time, but can actually hurt them in the future. When the company eventually seeks funding from investors that know what they are doing, the founder may find that he or she will have to accept a much lower valuation in order to secure the round. These lower valuations typically aren't "unfair," though...they're more reflective of where the company is in terms of product, market, and revenue. Nonetheless, they can come as a shock to those who have raised higher rounds previously.

NO MATERIAL CHANGES IN THE BUSINESS The purpose of raising capital in stages is to bring in the amount of money required to get your company to the next logical level (such as more customers, a pivoted product, or meaningful revenue generation). If you are not able to materially change your company's story – i.e. de-risk the opportunity to a point that makes the opportunity attractive to less risk-tolerant investors – you will most likely be forced to raise money at an equal or lesser valuation than your last raise. Investors with a higher risk tolerance will account for the risk in a high required rate of return, which could drive your valuation down (see Chapter 4 to review).

RAISE OR CLOSE Investors can sense desperation. If you are in a vulnerable position, where you will have to close down the business if you aren't able to obtain capital, potential investors will try and land on a valuation that gives them the maximum amount of equity without completely deflating the management team. However, they will likely seek to punish previous investors (more so than the founding team) by forcing those investors to take on a significant amount of dilution. This is known as a "cram down."

8.2 DILUTION FROM THE CRAM DOWN

If you remember from our discussion in Chapter 2, there are two types of dilution that can affect investors: **ownership-based dilution** and price-based dilution.

ownership-based dilution
an investor's ownership interest is diluted by the issuance of new equity

pre-emptive rights gives investors the ability invest in subsequent rounds to maintain their existing ownership

1. Most early-stage investors lack capital to participate in larger rounds and thus expect with ownership percentage to decrease somewhat over time.

Whereas ownership-based dilution decreases the ownership interest due to the issuance o new equity, price-based dilution decreases the value of the investor's ownership due to a funding event.

Investors expect that their percent ownership will decrease to some extent over time. Some investors hold **pre-emptive rights** (also referred to as pro-rata rights) to guard against this dilution; however, they must continually put more money into the company with each successive funding round in order to maintain their equity position.[1] Although dilution is somewhat expected, investors are never okay with a new investor coming in at a later stage and purchasing shares at a lower price.

Let's look at an example of down-round dilution to see what happens to early investors when a new investor comes in at a lower price:

EXAMPLE 8.1

Angel Dave purchases 200,000 shares at $1.00 per share in MealNow. With this investment, he acquires 20% of the total outstanding shares.

A year later, Tina the VC offers to invest $500,000 in MealNow in exchange for 40% of the company. What's the price per share Tina will pay, and how does this affect the value of Angel Dave's ownership?

Step 1: Determine the number of shares Tina will receive if the total number of outstanding shares is 1,000,000.

$$\text{New Equity Pool} = \frac{\text{Total Outstanding Shares}}{(1 - \text{Size of New Pool})} - \text{Total Outstanding Shares}$$

$$\text{New Equity Pool} = \frac{1,000,000}{(1 - .40)} - 1,000,000 = 666,667 \text{ shares}$$

Step 2: Determine the share price Tina will pay.

$$\text{Share Price} = \text{Investment} / \# \text{Shares}$$
$$\$500,000 / 666,667 \text{ shares} = \$0.75$$

Step 3: Determine the effect on Angel Dave.

Ownership-based dilution:

$$\text{New Ownership} = \text{Shares Held} / \text{Total Shares}$$
$$200,000 / 1,666,667 = 12\%$$

EXAMPLE 8.1 CONT.

Price-based dilution:

New Post-Money Valuation = Investment / Ownership %
$500,000 / 40% = $1,250,000

Value of Dave's ownership = $1,250,000 x 12% = $150,000

From this example, you can see that Angel Dave faces a significant decrease in both the amount of ownership he has in the company (decreased from 20% to 12%, an 8% difference), as well as the value of that ownership (decreased from $200,000 to $150,000, a 25% difference).

So, what can Angel Dave do to protect himself from these types of hits to ownership and equity? He can require anti-dilution provisions.

8.3 ANTI-DILUTION PROVISIONS

Anti-dilution provisions protect against price-based dilution (not ownership-based dilution). In the event of a down round, anti-dilution provisions trigger the issuance of additional shares to previous investors. The number of shares issued depends on the type of anti-dilution provision in play: full-ratchet or weighted average.

FULL-RATCHET ANTI-DILUTION

Full-ratchet anti-dilution provides "full-price" protection for the investor. Essentially, the original investor's shares will be automatically re-priced at the new valuation, and new shares will be issued to make the value commiserate with the initial investment.

anti-dilution provisions
the right of current shareholders to maintain their fractional ownership of a company by receiving a proportional number of shares of any future issue of common stock

full-ratchet anti-dilution
investor protection provision specifying that securities may be re-priced on par with the lowest price at which securities were issued

EXAMPLE 8.2

Continuing the example above, if Angel Dave had full-ratchet anti-dilution provisions, Sara must re-price Dave's investment so that he, too, acquires shares for $0.75 each. This will increase the amount of shares Dave holds.

Step 1: Calculate the number of shares Dave will acquire at the new price.

Original Investment / New Share Price = # Shares
$200,000 / $0.75 = 266,667 shares

Step 2: Subtract the original amount of shares Dave received.

266,667 - 200,000 = 66,667 new shares to be issued to Dave

Step 3: Prove that Dave received full price protection.

266,667 x $0.75 = $200,000

You can see that although Dave did not pay any more money into the company, he received new shares of stock to compensate him for the loss of value created by the down round. In other words, he received the exact number of shares to maintain the original value of his ownership, $200,000.

WEIGHTED AVERAGE ANTI-DILUTION

weighted average anti-dilution
average that takes into account the proportional relevance of each component of the issuance

In contrast to full-ratchet anti-dilution, **weighted average anti-dilution** provides for partial price protection. It takes into account the amount of capital that is raised, as well as the price at which the capital is raised.

Many times, founders complain about full-ratchet's automatic re-pricing. This is because the shares re-price regardless of how much capital is raised. Even if the amount of capital raised is minuscule and has no material impact on ownership dilution, each investor still gets re priced.

However, weighted average provisions account for this by using a formula that devises a weighted average price for the re-pricing that takes into account the amount of new capital raised.

EXAMPLE 8.3

If, instead, Dave had weighted-average provisions, Sara would come up with a weighted average price per share and restructure Dave's investment as if he had purchased shares at this new "fictitious" price. Keep in mind that, unlike full-ratchet anti-dilution, weighted-average anti-dilution provides only partial price protection. This partial price protection finds a balance between Dave's investment size (and price paid per share) and Tina's investment size (and price paid per share).

Step 1: Determine the weighted average price per share.

Total Cash Invested / Total Shares Owned = Weighted Average Price
($200,000 + $500,000) / (200,000 shares + 666,667 shares) = $0.81

Step 2: Determine the number of new shares issued to Dave.

Original Investment / Weighted Average Share Price = # Shares
$200,000 / $0.81 = 246,913 shares

246,913 - 200,000 = 46,913 new shares issued to Dave

Step 3: Find Dave's partial protection.

Total # Shares Held x New Price per Share
246,913 x $0.75 = $185,185

In this example, Angel Dave's value held dropped by approximately $15,000. While this isn't as satisfactory to investors as full-ratchet protection, it is better than no protection at all where Dave would have suffered a 25% drop in value.

EFFECT ON FOUNDERS, FAMILY, AND FRIENDS

When new shares are issued to old investors who hold anti-dilution provisions, the shares must be issued at the same time as the new investment. If these anti-dilution shares are issued after the new investment, they would dilute the new investor…not going to happen.

Because the shares will be issued alongside the new investment, the founders and management team will bear the brunt of ownership dilution (as well as anyone that participated in early rounds, such as friends and family).

Luckily, there is a silver lining: most investors realize that it's not in their best interest to cram down the people responsible for building the company (remember founders and managing team members must have an incentive for building the company). As such, it's not uncommon for later-stage investors to require earlier investors to back off their anti-dilution provisions. Alternatively, the later-stage investors may also find a way to bypass the provisions altogether through warrants.

As with most every other aspect of raising capital, dilution provisions can get complicated. It's best to have an attorney by your side throughout this process as complexity is introduced.

KEY TAKEAWAYS

- Down rounds can occur due to a variety of factors, ranging from macro-economic events to simply not materially advancing your startup.

- Down rounds can impact both ownership percentage and the value of ownership held.

- Investors can use anti-dilution provisions to protect their interests and cram down other parties that have previous ownership in the company.

CHAPTER 9
BUILDING WITH THE END IN MIND

Sara and Mike weren't completely sure what the "end" of MealNow would look like when they began it seven years ago. Heck, they barely knew what the beginning and middle were supposed to look like…how were they to know about exit potential?

However, they've learned a lot about what kinds of exits are desired through dealing with several groups of investors over the past few years. Now that they have acquisition offers on the table and a mass of loyal followers, it's time to delve deeper into exit strategies to see what types of implications they may have – not only on Sara and Mike as founders, but for their investors as well.

One of the fundamental needs of investors is an ability to exit an investment, as that enables them to recoup their investment plus any returns generated. If an investor isn't able to realize gains by liquidating their position in a company, what's the point of investing in the first place?

Investors typically prefer that the exit occur within a 5-7 year window, after the equity has appreciated significantly. Although there are "long-term" investors, they too must exit at some point.

Expect investors to seek rights within the investment agreement that will enable them to engineer and/or hasten an exit. The following sections give a brief summary of various types of exit opportunities and the corresponding rights investors may require in an investment agreement.

9.1 THE IPO

The most preferred exit option for an investor is an **initial public offering** of the company's stock, as it means that early investors will have likely achieved a 50-100x (or higher) return on their invested capital. It also gives them the ability to gradually sell their shares and liquidate their ownership position as they see fit.

initial public offering (IPO)
the first sale of stock by a company to the public

Although it may be the most desirable to investors, the hurdles to overcome before a company can achieve a successful IPO of its stock are significant. The primary challenge to a company pursing an IPO is building a book of investors that want to participate in the offering in a meaningful way (yes, going public is yet another round of fundraising). If there isn't enough interest, then the offering will be shelved and one liquidity option for investors is taken off the table. The company also must retain the services of an investment bank that will, in turn, advise the company as to whether or not there is an opportunity to go public, and if it would be worth going through the process (there are high costs to going through an IPO).

demand registration rights
gives an investor the ability to force a company to register its securities to be sold to the public, even against the wishes of the management

Occasionally, there is a large market desire for a private company to go public, even though the founders may want to keep the company private.[1] Investors, though, don't share the same concerns as the management team, and if there is an opportunity to IPO, they'll go after it. They see an opportunity to achieve liquidity for their investment, return large amounts of capital back to their limited partners, and launch new funds to invest in new businesses.

As a result, it is not uncommon to see an investor have **demand registration rights** in a company, giving the investor the ability to force the company to go public. While this doesn't assure that an IPO will be successful under any circumstance, it does give investors the ability to assert a huge amount of power if the market is asking for an IPO.

9.2 ACQUISITION

Short of an IPO, a strategic acquisition (preferably by a publically traded company or a company destined to go public) can drive huge returns for both investors and founders. In most instances, acquisition offers can be quickly vetted and a decision agreed upon by the

1. Although there could be promises of large returns, many companies want to stay private because of the requirements that come along with being publicly traded. It is expensive and time consuming to have to meet investor expectations every 90 days, and exhausting to have to answer to the public at large for any "controversial" decisions made.

drag along rights
allows majority
shareholders to
force minority
shareholders to ac-
cept an agreement

founding team and investors. However, on occasion, the investors will want to force an acquisition to occur (even without the founders' consent). They can achieve this through **drag along rights**.

For example, Tina the VC owns 40% of MealNow and wants to liquidate her position in the company after seven years. If she has drag along rights, she can proactively "shop" her ownership – as well as Sara's – to interested buyers! Most companies don't want to acquire a minority position in other companies…they want to own the whole company. Drag along rights give Tina the ability to find a buyer for the entire company without Sara's consent.

9.3 REDEMPTION RIGHTS

redemption
the return of an
investor's principal
in a security at or
prior to maturity

It is not uncommon to see an investor negotiate for the right to redeem their shares of the company, giving them the ability to cash out within a 5-7 year period. If a **redemption** (or **put option**) is exercised, the company must conduct a valuation of the investor's shares and come up with the cash to pay full value for the shares plus any accrued (but unpaid) dividends. Like going public, the company must have a good story to tell in order to raise the requisite capital to cash out existing investors.

put option
gives the holder
the right to sell
securities back to
the company at a
specified price

Although some of these provisions may seem to give investors too much control over the future of the company, it is important to remember that the process of raising capital is about investors lending you their money for a short period of time. They aren't ambivalent with respect to their options to exit when the time comes – they want to be certain that they'll get their money back (and then some).

All of these rights put the management team on the clock in terms of value acceleration which can actually be a good thing! You probably already know that a 7-10 year period is a long time in the start-up world. As you experience business and make connections throughout various industries, you'll probably also become interested in a wide variety of things and want to explore business in those areas.

If you run the business with the expectation of an exit, it puts you in the mindset of creating as much value as possible within a condensed timeframe. Much to the pleasure of your investors, you'll drive that much harder to an exit, just so you can start this crazy process all over again.

KEY TAKEAWAYS

- An investor's primary interest lies in finding the fastest and most profitable way to exit a company. Be prepared for investment agreements that give him or her various types of exit rights.

- Every startup investor dreams of an IPO – but your company may be better suited for other harvest scenarios (such as an acquisition).

- If you build the company with a mindset of value acceleration, investors will be ready and willing to help drive the company to an exit.

CHAPTER 10
GETTING THE DEAL DONE:
FINDING COMMON GROUND IN NEGOTIATIONS

Now that they understand the ins and outs of various types of equity, control provisions, and what investors expect out of a deal, Mike and Sara are ready to fully enter equity negotiations with interested investors.

Unfortunately, knowing the basics of equity types isn't enough to make them shrewd negotiators – there are many ways that deals can play out based on the way that all of the various components interact. As such, it would be wise for them to sit down and construct a set of deals with different combinations of terms - and work through the scenarios fully - to learn more about the interplay of deal components.

Throughout this book, we've discussed what is involved in the process of selling equity to investors from a variety of standpoints, including calculations you can use to help you hold on to your equity, as well as the softer nuances of what investors might want or expect to see in the deal terms.

In this chapter, we'll bring all of the information together with tangible strategies that can help during your negotiations, focusing on different types of leverage you may be able to utilize, as well as creative strategies to help you and your investors find common ground when you can't seem to agree on anything.

10.1 USE MARKET TIMING TO YOUR ADVANTAGE

In previous chapters, we've talked about how macroeconomic factors can play into things like dilution and valuation. It stands to reason, then, that the economic climate during which you seek capital will have a huge impact on the deal that you negotiate with an investor. Although you cannot predict, dictate, or change the macroeconomic climate, you must be aware of the state of the market as a whole in order to better understand how and when to approach investors (and adjust your expectation for funding terms accordingly).

bullish market
a prolonged period in which investment prices rise faster than their historical average; can be a result of an economic recovery or "boom"

If at all possible, only pursue funding in a **bullish market** climate. Bullish climates are more favorable to entrepreneurs because actual and perceived risks to investors are lower. During these times of economic "booms," capital is more prevalent in the marketplace. Because more capital is available, entrepreneurs typically have more options for funding as investors compete to fund deals. This is referred to as "money chasing the deal." As you can guess, if the money is chasing you, that's a good thing!

bearish market
a prolonged period in which investment prices fall accompanied by widespread pessimism; usually during a recession

Conversely, be cautious about trying to raise money in a **bearish market** climate. Bear markets are the opposite of bull markets; during these times, capital is short and investors are risk-averse, making it difficult to raise money at a valuation you think your company might deserve. To have the best shot at protecting your equity, try to start and bootstrap your company during bear markets and only raise capital when bull market conditions are present. Table 10.1 helps to further depict how the market conditions may influence your deal terms with investors.

However, if you are in the position where your company is running out of money and you need to raise capital to stay open, the market climate probably won't be of much help to you – this is one of the worst situations to be in as a founder.

When investors know you need their money to survive, you are at a severe disadvantage in the negotiations. The only real way to negate it is if multiple investors want to invest in your company.

Many times, the only way out of this situation is to accept the investment terms and structure that the investor offers…or be forced to close your business. If this is the case for you, your primary concern – and primary point of leverage – must be to make sure that you and your team have enough incentive to continue to build the company. If the investor will not grant you that, you have some very important decisions to consider before accepting.

TABLE 10.1

	Bear Market Short Supply of $	Bull Market Heavy Supply of $
Negotiation Advantage	Investor	Entrepreneur
Investor's Aversion to Risk	High	Low
Investor's Preference on Stage	Later Stages	Earlier Stages
Investor's Tendency to Invest in New Deals	Low	High
Average Investment Size	Lower	Higher
Average Valuation	Lower	Higher
Frequency of Down Rounds & Cram Downs	Higher	Lower
Anti-Dilution Provisions	Full Ratchet	Weighted Average
Type of Security	Participating Preferred	Convertible Preferred
Control Provisions	Less Flexible	More Flexible

10.2 PUT ON YOUR GREEN HAT

In Edward de Bono's theory of the Six Thinking Caps, the green hat represents creativity. While investment and funding decisions may seem like cut and dry calculations involving returns and payback periods, the truth of the matter is that structuring deals is an art – you must put on your "green hat" and get a little creative in order to effectively structure a deal that works for both you and your investor.

While each party can have the tendency to get stuck on particular deal terms, those terms can oftentimes be worked out with a little creative thinking. If you understand how the various deal terms work together, you can adjust the terms as if they were levers in order to find a structure that makes sense for both sides.

Let's look at a few examples of how various terms might interact to build a deal that both sides find favorable:

VALUATION

Valuation, as we know, is always going to be a difficult negotiation because nobody knows the true value – present or future – of a company. Typically, you'll view your company as having bigger potential than an investor will, and you'll need to figure out how to "close the gap" in the valuation discussion.

There are several ways to do this through tweaking share type and return preference multiples alone. Generally, you'll need to lower the risk and downside for the investor in order to offset a higher valuation on the deal. Here are a few ways to do just that:

Participating Preferred Shares + High Return Preference = Higher Valuation

Convertible Preferred Shares w/ High Return Preference = Higher Valuation

Full-Ratchet Anti-Dilution Provisions can be traded for a Higher Valuation

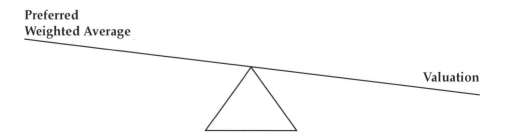

Offer participating preferred shares with full-ratchet
anti-dilution provisions to increase valuation.

Be willing to accept a lower valuation in exchange for
preferred shares and / or weighted average anti-dilution.

Conversely, if you are set on offering preferred shares and weighted average anti-dilution (instead of offering full price protection), you may have to take a hit on valuation.

As with anything, valuation negotiations are give-and-take. You need to be aware of the terms that offset one another, so you can offer deal terms that make sense and achieve the outcome you desire. Revisit Chapter 6 to understand how to calculate waterfalls...it would be highly beneficial to work through various scenarios to better see how structure type can affect payouts.

Let's walk through a few scenarios here as well to see how various combinations of deal terms can play out.

EXAMPLE 10.1

Sara is negotiating with Tina the VC on valuation. Tina offers to invest $1,000,000 at a post money valuation of $2,500,000 in the form of a convertible preferred security. Sara believes the post-money valuation should be $4,000,000.

> Step 1: Calculate the difference in equity Tina will receive in MealNow at the two valuations.
>
> Investment / Post-Money Valuation = Equity Ownership
> $1,000,000 / $4,000,000 = 25% ownership
> $1,000,000 / $2,500,000 = 40% ownership
>
> Step 2: Calculate the difference in payout Tina will receive if MealNow is sold for $100MM valuation vs. a $20MM valuation.
>
> If Tina does not exercise her option to convert into common shares, she will receive her investment at 1x return preference payout, no matter what the outcome. If she converts her shares into common equity, she will receive:
>
> $100MM x 25% = $25,000,000
> $100MM x 40% = $40,000,000
>
> $20MM x 25% = $5,000,000
> $20MM x 40% = $8,000,000

As you can see, if Sara builds the company to a $100MM valuation, the extra 15% of equity is significant. However, if the deal peters out at a $20MM valuation, Tina needs the extra 15% to eek out a return for her fund.

How can Sara and Tina bridge the gap on valuation in order to strike a deal each of them is comfortable with?

EXAMPLE 10.2

One potential solution for Sara to offer is that Tina could invest $1,000,000 in MealNow at a post-money valuation of $3,500,000 with participating preferred shares that have a 2x

EXAMPLE 10.2 CONT.

return preference.

To see how this works, let's revisit the $100MM vs. $20MM exits.

Step 1: Calculate Tina's ownership at the new investment level.

Investment / Post-Money Valuation = Equity Ownership
$1,000,000 / $3,500,000 = 28.57% ownership

Step 2: Calculate Tina's return on a $100,000,000 exit.

Return preference = 2 x $1,000,000 investment = $2,000,000

(Buyout Price - Return Preference) x % Ownership
($100,000,000 - $2,000,000) x 28.57% = $28,000,000

$2,000,000 + $28,000,000 = $30,000,000 received at payout

$30,000,000 / $100,000,000 = **30% of total payout**

Step 3: Calculate Tina's return on a $20,000,000 exit.

Return preference = 2 x $1,000,000 investment = $2,000,000

(Buyout Price - Return Preference) x % Ownership
($20,000,000 - $2,000,000) x 28.57% = $5,142,600

$2,000,000 + $5,142,600 = $7,142,600 received at payout

$7,142,600 / $20,000,000 = **35.7% of total payout**

When comparing the above scenarios, you can see that if the exit is small ($20,000,000), Tina will get a bigger chunk of the proceeds by holding participating preferred shares with a return preference as opposed to in the convertible preferred scenario. If the exit is big, not only will Tina get a nice return but Sara gets to enjoy a larger return as well.

Another path Sara could have chosen is to suggest that Tina receive convertible preferred shares with an outsized return preference (i.e. 3x) OR the right to convert into common equity.

Finally, as shown in the illustrations above, Sara could agree to full-ratchet anti-dilution in any of the scenarios in exchange for a higher valuation. This would ensure that Tina receives full price protection in the event of a future down round.

There are dozens of ways to configure an equity deal to suit both parties – you now have a number of "tools in the toolbox" that can allow you to creatively practice and structure deal terms. The more you understand how these terms work together, and the more you understand the needs of the party you're negotiating with, the more creative you can be in finding common ground.

Convertible notes can accelerate the process of getting cash into the company in the early stages, enabling you to concentrate on building the business sooner. Since these types of investments typically happen early in the life of a startup, it is usually less of a negotiation process than raising equity capital. However, there is room to negotiate a bit on discount rates and capped valuations.

10.3 BEING REASONABLE

"To be...or not to be? That is the question." We've heard it again and again...and yes, this age-old question applies to equity financings.

There are a couple of schools of thought when it comes to negotiating a deal: should you be reasonable or gutsy in your requests?

One doctrine is to ask for terms unreasonably in your favor, knowing that you have room to come down in several areas and still be satisfied with the deal. Others, however, believe that it is best to be completely transparent, with a clear and firm position on what you're asking for (and reasons to back it up).

Unfortunately, there is no right answer here. Remember what we said about getting inside the minds of the investors you are courting? If you understand the person and their motivations, it will help point you towards an appropriate strategy. Additionally, you must understand that after the negotiations are over, you and your company's investors are partners. Both sides must have the potential to win in the deal for a deal to be struck in the first place.

KEY TAKEAWAYS

- Timing the market plays a large role in helping you to get favorable deal terms – try and raise money only during bull markets and bootstrap in a bearish market climate.

- There are multiple ways to structure deal terms that please both founders and investors...but sometimes, you have to get a little creative.

- Figure out a strategy for your "ask" that you are comfortable with. There is no one strategy that always works, so know what you need out of the deal and approach investors confidently regardless of the strategy that you pick!

IT'S TIME TO GET STARTED

We wrote this book to give you a high-level overview of founder's equity. We hope that it will help you better manage the process of distributing equity to co-founders, employees, and investors. More importantly, we designed *The First-Time Founder's Equity Bible* to help you take the emotions out of the equity distribution process.

Remember, the minute you distribute equity to others, the business is no longer exclusively yours…you cannot run the company as if it is your baby. If you do so, you run the risk of getting out of sync with your investors and burning many bridges in the process.

If, however, you think of your company as a collaboration of many, you can use equity as a valuable tool to align high-caliber individuals around the goal of building something of true worth. The key to doing so is creating an effective distribution model for you, your co-founders, employees, and investors. After that, building a high-potential venture becomes as fun and rewarding as it is challenging.

To repeat a statement often used in this book, you are strongly encouraged to seek the advice of counsel during the process of raising equity. This book is not designed to teach you how to execute equity transactions. Many investors, attorneys, and consultants may have their own valuation models, terminologies, and approaches when it comes to equity. However, the underlying principals of this book will allow you to quickly decipher their methodologies, as well as work up models of your own so you are able to enter discussions with an idea of how the negotiation process may play out.

Take the time to understand the obligations that come with raising equity capital from investors – we hope you can see that it is not a process to be taken lightly. Additionally, it is important that you understand the scale to which you need to build your company in order for you and your co-founders to realize a return on your time and talent.

Going into the equity distribution process with your eyes wide open will serve you well and allow you structure win/win deals for everyone involved. We hope that, through this book, we have given you the tools to do just that.

Good Luck!

GLOSSARY

accelerator - (p 38) privately-funded early stage investment fund that supports entrepreneurs with funding, mentoring, training, development events, and access to a premier investor network for a definite period of time in exchange for equity

accrued dividends - (p 66) dividend that is considered to be earned but not declared or payable

anchoring - (p 41) tendency to rely too heavily on certain pieces of information when making decisions

angel investors - (p 39) wealthy individuals operating as informal or private investors who provide venture financing for small businesses

anti-dilution provisions - (p 79) the right of current shareholders to maintain their fractional ownership of a company by receiving a proportional number of shares of any future issue of common stock

bartering - (p 38) type of trading in which goods or services are exchanged without the use of cash, used in times of high inflation or tight money

bearish market - (p 86) a prolonged period in which investment prices fall accompanied by widespread pessimism; usually during a recession

bias - (p 41) inclination or preference that influences judgment from being balanced

board of directors - (p 21) governing body of a firm. The members are elected by the shareholders and have ultimate decision-making authority

bootstrap - (p 38) building a business out of very little or virtually nothing, keeping costs as low as possible and relying on personal income or savings, sweat equity, low operating costs, fast inventory turnaround; avoiding outside investors so ownership is not diluted

bullish market - (p 86) a prolonged period in which investment prices rise faster than their historical average; can be a result of an economic recovery or "boom"

burn rate - (p 45) speed at which a new firm consumes capital and credit before breaking even and generating income

c-corp - (p 60) business that is a completely separate tax entity from its owners (unlike a partnership)

capitalization table - (p 21) shows who owns what in the company, listing the company's shareholders, the amount of shares they hold, and how much they paid for those shares, in order of decreasing liquidity preference

class of equity - (p 65) types of equity that have different attributes, characteristics, or payof benefits

competitive risk - (p 46) the risk that a company cannot ward off competitors before it car return capital to investors

confirmation bias - (p 41) tendency to retain only what conforms to one's preferences and reject that which does not

convertible note - (p 34) structured as a loan at the time of investment; outstanding balance is automatically converted to equity when a later equity investor appears

convertible preferred stock - (p 27) shares which can be exchanged for another related secu rity (i.e. common shares) at the option of the holder

convertible with a cap - (p 35) debt-like investment instrument that converts into equity ir the future at a discount to the funding price with a pre-set price maximum

cross the chasm - (p 37) gaining market share as the company moves from acquiring / serv ing early adopters to mainstream consumers

cumulative dividends - (p 68) dividends that are an obligation regardless of the earnings o the company. Must be paid before any common stock dividends

de-risking - (p 37) process of a creating enough certainty in your company such that it be comes an attractive opportunity to a large pool of investors

dead equity - (p 62) equity held by employees and founders no longer working at the com pany

debt capital - (p 33) borrowing someone else's money to finance the business under the con dition that the money (plus interest accrued) must be paid back in full by an agreed upor date in the future

defensible - (p 37) meaningful differentiation in product sets to gain market share, expanc margins and keep competitors at bay; ex: competitive advantage, barriers to entry, IP, lan guage

demand registration rights - (p 83) gives an investor the ability to force a company to regis ter its securities to be sold to the public, even against the wishes of the management

dilution - (p 23) occurs for any event that requires the company to issue more shares; equity stake decreases in proportion to the percent of the company new investors buy

down round - (p 24) when a company raises money at a lower valuation or share price thar in a previous round; existing shareholders lose value

drag along rights - (p 84) allows majority shareholders to force minority shareholders to accept an agreement

equity - (p 16) the value of ownership in a property, i.e. a business

equity capital - (p 33) represents the risk capital staked by investors through investment in the company

founder's shares - (p 16) shares of stock that are issued to the founders of a firm

full-ratchet anti-dilution - (p 79) investor protection provision specifying that securities may be re-priced on par with the lowest price at which securities were issued

fully-diluted - (p 21) calculation of the shareholder's percent ownership after all possible shares have been issued

future value - (p 49) the sum to which today's investment will grow by a specific future date when compounded at a given interest rate

hold times - (p 47) the time between the date of the purchase of an asset and the date of the sale of the asset

initial public offering (IPO) - (p 83) the first sale of stock by a company to the public

lien - (p 33) a legal claim to another person's property

liquidation preference - (p 25) the order in which creditors are paid off if the business is liquidated

liquidity event - (p 34) the way in which an investor plans to close out an investment; i.e. an exit strategy. For example, an IPO or acquisition

liquidity risk - (p 44) probability of loss arising from a situation where there will not be enough cash or cash equivalents to meet debts; sale of illiquid assets will yield less than their fair value

macro risk - (p 46) large-scale economic factors that you cannot control (and oftentimes cannot predict) that affect your business in a negative way

management risk - (p 46) the risks associated with ineffective, destructive or underperforming management, which hurt shareholders and the company or fund being managed. In this situation, the company would be better off without the choices made by management

market risk - (p 45) probability of loss common to all businesses and investment opportunities and inherent in all dealings in a market

optimism bias - (p 41) tendency to overestimate favorable outcomes

option pool - (p 28) shares set aside for possible issuance to employees at a later date

ownership-based dilution - (p 77) an investor's ownership interest is diluted by the issuance of new equity

participating preferred shares - (p 67) shareholders' payouts include the initial amount invested, dividends, and a conversion into common stock

pass-through - (p 60) a firm's owners pay income tax on the firm's income and not the firm

platform business - (p 49) businesses that allow users to create and consume value, i.e. users (producers) can create value on the platform for other users (consumers) to consume. Ex Facebook, Twitter, YouTube, and Google

pre-emptive rights - (p 78) gives investors the ability invest in subsequent rounds to maintain their existing ownership

preferred shares - (p 65) dividends are paid before anything is paid to common stock holders in the event of a liquidation

price-based dilution - (p 24) the value of the investor's ownership has decreased due to a funding event; when shares of stock are sold at a price per share that is less than the price paid by earlier investors

price per share - (p 51) determines how many shares an investor can buy for a given dollar investment

pro-rata - (p 17) proportionate allocation of a quantity on the basis of one common factor (ex profit is divided among stockholders on the basis of how many shares each holds)

promissory note - (p 34) document signed by a borrower promising to repay a loan under agreed-upon terms

put option - (p 84) gives the holder the right to sell securities back to the company at a specified price

qualified financing - (p 34) an equity financing in which a minimum amount of capital is raised

rate of return - (p 44) expressed as a percentage of the total amount invested

redemption - (p 84) the return of an investor's principal in a security at or prior to maturity

repurchase agreement - (p 17) agreement allowing the startup to buy back ownership at a later date for a nominal amount

retention ratio - (p 50) a backend calculation that helps to determine how much equity to request

return preference - (p 65) often listed in multiples of the original investment amount

scale - (p 49) if gaining additional revenue requires relatively smaller and smaller additions of operating costs, your business is scalable

Series A - (p 39) a company's first significant round of traditional venture capital

share price - (p 25) same as price paid per share; in successful companies, it increases as the company becomes more valuable

strike price - (p 28) the price at which an option is exercisable

valuation - (p 44) appraisal or estimate of the worth of the business

vesting - (p 17) the accrual of non-forfeitable rights to ownership over a pre-determined period of time

veto - (p 74) the right to stop an action

waterfall scenario - (p 69) specifies the order of distribution to investors upon a liquidity event

weighted average anti-dilution - (p 80) average that takes into account the proportional relevance of each component of the issuance

ENDNOTES

i.   http://www.crunchbase.com/company/instagram - p 13

ii.   http://whoownsfacebook.com/ - p 16

iii.   http://www.kauffman.org/newsroom/number-of-us-companies-that-reach-100-million-dollars-in-annual-revenues-remarkably-stable over-past-20-years-according-to-kauffman-paper.aspx - p 16

iv.   The following resources are helpful in seeing a range of viewpoints in the debate over convertible notes - p 36:

        http://cdixon.org/2010/08/31/converts-versus-equity-deals/

        http://cdixon.org/2009/08/12/why-seed-investors-dont-like-convertible-notes/

        http://www.bothsidesofthetable.com/2010/08/30/is-convertible-debt-preferable-to-equity/

        http://www.sethlevine.com/wp/2010/08/has-convertible-debt-won-and-if-it-has-is-that-a-good-thing

        http://www.bothsidesofthetable.com/2012/09/05/the-truth-about-convertible-debt-at-startups-and-the-hidden-terms-you-didnt-understand/

v.   http://mashable.com/2012/10/17/color-shuts-down/ - p 38

vi.   http://www.theverge.com/2013/9/3/4688888/there-will-never-be-another-nokia-smartphone - p 45

vii.   http://www.theverge.com/2013/9/3/4690534/what-exactly-did-microsoft-just-buy-from-nokia-a-visual-guide/in/4453001 - p 45

viii.   http://www.turtleweb.com/turtleweb.nsf/list4lookup/marketinfo?opendocument - p 49

ix.   A few beginning thoughts and resources on how to tell your story - p 50:

        Made to Stick by Chip Heath and Dan Heath

        http://cdixon.org/2010/04/03/size-markets-using-narratives-not-numbers/

        http://avc.com/2010/06/six-slides/

        http://bothsidesofthetable.com/2009/06/06/the-first-vc-meeting-post-1-of-many/ (click through the full series)

ix.   continued...

http://sethgodin.typepad.com/seths_blog/2006/04/ode_how_
to_tell.html

x.   http://en.wikipedia.org/wiki/First_Chicago_Method - p 52

xi.   http://www.vcmethod.com/ - p 52

xii.   http://www.feld.com/wp/archives/2012/05/vc-rights-up-down-and-
know-what-the-fuck-is-going-on.html - p 62

(also see: http://avc.com/2009/04/the-three-terms-you-must-
have-in-a-venture-investmemt/)

Made in the USA
Columbia, SC
21 August 2018